ROWAN WILLIAMS IN CONVERSATION

Rowan Williams and Greg Garrett

T0339133

Originally published in the United States of America in 2019 by Church Publishing, 19 East 34th Street, New York, NY 10016

First published in Great Britain in 2020

Society for Promoting Christian Knowledge
36 Causton Street
London SW1P 4ST
www.spck.org.uk

Copyright © Rowan Williams and Greg Garrett, 2019, 2020

All rights reserved. No part of this book may be reproduced or transmitted in any form or by any means, electronic or mechanical, including photocopying, recording, or by any information storage and retrieval system, without permission in writing from the publisher.

SPCK does not necessarily endorse the individual views contained in its publications.

Scripture quotations are taken from the New Revised Standard Version of the Bible, copyright © 1989 by the Division of Christian Education of the National Council of the Churches of Christ in the USA. Used by permission. All rights reserved.

British Library Cataloguing-in-Publication Data
A catalogue record for this book is available from the British Library

ISBN 978–0–281–08371–8
eBook ISBN 978–0–281–08372–5

First printed in Great Britain by Jellyfish Print Solutions
Subsequently digitally printed in Great Britain

eBook by Manilla Typesetting Company

Produced on paper from sustainable forests

Contents

Foreword

WHEN NANCY BRYAN, who commissioned this book for the In Conversations series, first spoke to me about it in her Manhattan office several years ago, I smiled and said it sounded like a lovely idea. Rowan Williams and I have been having enjoyable and, for me, certainly, transformational talks for over a decade, and more than once I have had other friends say they'd love to be a fly on the wall for our conversations. I mentioned Nancy's offer to Rowan in an e-mail, and said I thought it might be fun. But I also thought it unlikely ever to happen, as you would be hard-pressed to find two people with more things to write than Rowan and myself. But Nancy persisted, sat down with Rowan at the University of the South during his stateside visit there in fall 2016, and talked him into doing this book.

The idea behind the In Conversation series is very simple: two friends who happen to be theologians come together to talk about their lives, their spiritual practices, the Church, their passions. In the process, readers are permitted to be flies on the wall as the speakers reflect on matters that are personal but also of universal importance. When the first book in the series came out in 2017, it set a high bar, featuring, as it did, two trailblazers, the Most Rev. Michael Curry, the first African American presiding bishop of the American Episcopal Church, and Barbara Harris, the first female bishop elected in the entire Anglican Communion, as well as the first African American bishop in the Episcopal Church. Bishops Harris and Curry talked about their long friendship, their history with the Church, social justice, and what it felt like to constantly be the "first" something. Their lives have been remarkable—Bishop Harris marched with

Dr. King and Bishop Curry recently electrified the world by preaching Jesus at a certain royal wedding—and they ushered in the series with distinction.

To follow such dynamic leaders, thinkers, and preachers, I suppose Nancy thought only a Rowan Williams would do. Although he is not the sort of person to delight in such praise, Rowan is not only the past archbishop of Canterbury, the spiritual leader of some eighty million Anglican Christians around the world, but was recognized even before his term as archbishop as one of the world's best and most important theologians. I would listen to Rowan Williams talk about cleaning the oven or baking bread—two things we do in fact talk about in these conversations. He has written marvelous books on the Church and Christian belief, on literature, on Christian spiritual practices, on Christian traditions, and much more. I first encountered Rowan in 2004 as a seminarian reading *On Christian Theology* (2000) in my first semester at the Episcopal Seminary of the Southwest. The density of his thought, the intricacy of his reasoning, the construction of his arguments, and the beauty of his language floored me; he became my favorite theologian, and remains so to this day. When he wrote in his essay "The Judgment of the World" in that collection that "all good stories change us if we hear them attentively; the most serious stories change us radically" (42), he was expressing my own long-held but newly theological belief that story—whether novel, film, or powerful personal experience—offered the keys to transformation.

As a novelist, memoirist, and film critic, I had come to seminary to learn new kinds of writing, and to understand how the writing I had been doing could have a sacred value. When I discovered Rowan's *Grace and Necessity: Reflections on Art and Love* (2005), a book about the Southern writer Flannery O'Connor, with whom I have always felt a strong connection, and the Welsh poet and painter David Jones, he showed me that story and culture were most definitely vehicles for spiritual meaning. Here was the archbishop of Canterbury and my favorite Christian theologian demonstrating that films, music, and other forms of culture could be taken as seriously as I cared to take them. While I'd cowritten, in addition to my novels, a book on *The Matrix* films and a book on the spiritual themes of comics and graphic novels, *Grace and Necessity* encouraged me to go deeper, to think more seriously about the relationship between the supposedly secular and the sacred, and what followed for me were a book on Hollywood film structured as systematic theology, a book on grief exploring archetypal narratives for their meanings, and a book on the rock band U2 exploring the theological dimensions of their songs, of their work for peace and justice, and of their life together as a sacred community.

I was discovering that my fiction, my spiritual autobiography, and my work as a cultural theologian were all linked through the desire to make meaning, to understand why we are here, to what we are called, what the basic shape of the universe might be, and what might be at the heart of it. It was at about this time that, as we relate, Rowan began reading my work, beginning with the first edition of my spiritual autobiography, *Crossing Myself*. I still have Rowan's letter from Lambeth Palace dated October 25, 2006, in which he described having to tear himself away from reading it to get on with other work. (That I almost didn't receive his letter—and that our friendship thus might have never happened—boggles my mind.) But I did, and we became first pen pals, sharing thoughts on each other's latest work, and then, eventually, friends meeting face-to-face to share a cup of tea or a meal and to talk about the writers we admired and the families we loved.

Rowan's encouragement of my work as novelist, memoirist, and cultural theologian was important to me early in my career, and continues to be important to this day. (You can hear his encouragement in the conversation you're about to read, just as I hope you hear my encouragement to Rowan to continue to create as a poet and playwright, two forms in which I wish more people knew his work.) Now when we meet for conversation, we do so on slightly more level ground, for there are things I have learned to do well, and gaps for each of us completed in some way by the other. When I ask him about his prayer practice—or he asks me about reading popular culture for spiritual meaning—there is genuine curiosity, growing I suppose out of the recognition that the other has helpful knowledge.

But in this conversation, most importantly, I hope you hear two friends who delight in each other's company, and who find their imaginations fired by the exchange of ideas themselves. I had told people that what Rowan and I do when we get together is talk; what you will read in the pages that follow is the proof of that, but also the value of it. As I said, I would listen to Rowan talk about bread rising, and even though we revisited topics we had discussed many times, I learned much from the three days in July 2018 we spent in Rowan's study in Cambridge, where he is master of Magdalene College. I hope this conversation inspired new thoughts for Rowan as well; as I've listened again to the audio files, I'm struck by how often one of us responds to the other with "yes," or "of course," or a laugh, or a grunt of recognition, or by completing the other's thought. These conversations were good for the two of us, which suggests to me that there will be something here for you as well, whether you're interested in the practice of prayer, or how Christians are called to approach politics, or how we write, or what happens when we write well, or how Shakespeare teaches us to be more human, or the preaching event, or why Doctor Who deserves his own "Gospel According To" book.

Who will be interested in this book? Since it ranges so widely, I like to think a wide range of people will be drawn to this, one of the most thoughtful and interesting conversations in which I've ever participated. If you're interested in the Church, you have the chance to listen in as a past archbishop of Canterbury and an enthusiastic convert to the Episcopal Church talk about what the Church is called to be doing and how it can make a difference in the life of the world. If you're a writer, teacher, preacher, or avid reader, you get to hear two writers and teachers talking about form and practice, discussing works that have shaped their own lives and work, and noting some of the connections between the writing practice of a poet, fiction writer, or public theologian and the weekly work of a preacher. If, in fact, you must preach every Sunday, you'll be pleased, I hope, to hear a professional writer and one of the world's greatest theologians admit how hard it is to preach well and to confess our own failures. If you care about the ways God's revelation is still being experienced in the world—the idea of epiphany, of God's continuous showing-forth, is a constant refrain in these conversations—then you'll hearken with interest to the comments on literature and culture and how they help us make meaning. If you're a person seeking a deeper practice or experience of faith, you'll find discussion here of how to pray, how to listen, and of how to show up for God. If, as my friends used to say, you'd just like to listen in when Rowan and I talk about what we care about, what the Church is for, and what we're supposed to be doing in life, then this is also a place you'll find welcome and comfort. I've been continuously engaged and excited about these talks while revisiting them, and we both hope that they might be a source of insight, inspiration, and delight for you as well.

A few notes on how this work was edited. Rowan and I envisioned this book as a sort of public conversation, something each of us has done often, where you are speaking and listening to another person onstage, but at the same time, must remain aware that what you're saying is intended for a larger audience. This book mostly consists of the words that Rowan and I first spoke to each other in his study in Cambridge, and it remains intentionally more oral than written, although I have edited lightly for clarity and readability. It also meanders, in that way that good conversations do, incorporating what has gone before, branching out into new directions. We felt that this was a form that worked, where you could hear us circle back around to the things that drive us, whether the novel *Gilead,* or the plays of Shakespeare, or the work and practice of writers and theologians. I've also included some parenthetical notes to help you follow more easily, or track down some of the writers or passages we consider in these pages. I have not attempted to summarize Rowan's works (or mine) when they're discussed here, because often we provide context in the discussion itself, and anyway, there's too damn many books for anyone to keep straight. I'm exhausted just looking up the publication information!

In the pages that follow, you'll be privy to two friends excitedly returning to topics they've discussed many times, yet having flashes of new insight in the process. We enjoyed having the talks you'll read here, and could have gone right on talking, which may be the greatest testimony to the transformational power of conversation. For Rowan and myself, I offer this prayer: may this book spark some excited conversations and new thoughts of your own, may it, above all, be useful, and may the blessing of that One who is constantly revealed to us as the God of love, compassion, and inspiration be with you, now and always.

Grace and peace,
Greg Garrett
Ordinary Time,
2018
Austin, TX

Conversation One

In Which Rowan and Greg Discuss: Friendship / Being Archbishop of Canterbury / The Practice of Prayer / Intention and Attention / Celtic Christianity / Welsh and Celtic Writers / Being Present / Cooking and Singing as Spiritual Practices

RW: I think perhaps we might begin by telling people how we met. It's my recollection that you sent me a manuscript.

GG: Right. I think it was actually the galley version of *Crossing Myself* [1st edition 2006].

RW: I think that's it, yes.

GG: You may remember that you sent a letter in care of the publisher, and the story I'm fond of telling is that this was not a Christian publisher with much familiarity with the Anglican tradition. They called me to say, "You received a letter from London, and we thought we might just throw it away, but it's from someone Williams, someone Williams in a palace somewhere in London." "Rowan Williams?" I said. "Yes," they said. "That's it. How did you know?"

Oh, two and two. I put them together.

RW: Williams. Palace.

GG: Yes. So our early friendship was conducted through the mail, so to speak, and my recollection is that the first time we met face-to-face I was staying at Canterbury and working in the library on, I think, the U2 book [*We Get to Carry Each Other*, 2009].

RW: That rings a bell.

GG: And you had invited me up to Lambeth Palace for tea and that was the first time we met.

RW: My recollection is that we talked that first time about novels. I was very fascinated by your record as a novelist. And we talked a great deal about who the novelists were who were worth looking at in the UK and in the United States at that point.

GG: We had several folks in common, and of course Marilynne Robinson's *Gilead* [2004] is a sort of foundational text for both of us. I'm sure we'll come back to that again at some point. I do remember talking a lot with Mary [Whitticase], your PA, a lovely, lovely woman, and because I am from the States and was a recent convert to the Episcopal Church, there was a lot I didn't know about what one does when one meets the archbishop of Canterbury, which of course you were at the time. But Mary put all my fears to rest. I asked her everything about dress code and everything else, and her response essentially was just, "Come. All will be well." I remember thinking afterward what a lovely meeting we had. We talked about books, we talked a bit about our families, and we sort of established from that very first meeting we didn't talk about what we called "The Day Job." I don't know if that was something that was good for you—

RW: It was something very important to me. All through my time those years, it mattered greatly to have people I could talk to who write at an angle to the Day Job. The problems of the Anglican Communion during those years don't need elaboration. It was a daily source of prayer and concern. But I had to remind myself all the time that the only thing that made sense of any of that was what it was for. What the Church existed for. What ministries in the church existed for. And that was, really, to let the world know something. And if you didn't have friends and conversations which reminded what the world needed to know, then frankly the rest would just be insanity. It was fairly insane as it was.

One of the things that kept it from tipping over into complete absurdity. So, yes, just as I found it very important in those years myself to be writing a bit, to have events that had nothing to do with ecclesiastical negotiations and politics. Just as when I had that sabbatical in 2007, I went and wrote that book on Dostoevsky [*Dostoevsky: Language, Faith, and Fiction*, 2008], which shocked a lot of people. It was all part of the same thing. I personally needed to keep that perspective. I know a lot of people thought that if I took a sabbatical I should spend it writing position papers for the Lambeth Conference. Mysteriously, I didn't find that quite such an attractive prospect. It was good that I had the chance to step back to think about all those issues we talk about so often, the interweaving of faith and imagination.

GG: It was funny, because we are both Church People. I was finishing seminary at that time and just starting on my vocation as a writer and speaker in the larger church. Whenever people found out that you and I were friends, they would ask me a lot of policy questions and would ask me, "Do you ever talk with him about this?" and I told them, "No. We don't really talk about any of that." We talk about this shared work that we love and the ways that art and culture help us to do the work that we love.

RW: And vice versa. Because it seems to me that when we talk about the relationship between faith and art and culture it's not that being a person of religious faith makes you a better writer or being a good writer helps you have a religious faith. But somehow the two of them feed and prod and stimulate each other. All the time.

GG: As the friendship developed, we went from having an hour's coffee together to spending weekends together, and I came to think of you as a very dear friend. To think of you, even though we were only seeing each other in person, you know, once or twice a year, as present in my life, as you do with good friends. I'm sure you remember occasions where I would be in touch and say, "Here is something that is going on in my life, I'd like you to pray with me about this," really a couple of huge decisions I faced over the last decade.

RW: And I felt a great privilege in being invited to share that, and certainly I and the family came to regard you as very much a friend, a humanizing presence for us. My son [Pip] has said more than once that it was nice to have someone coming to stay with us who talked to him as a human being, not just to his father.

GG: Oh, I love Pip. You have a wonderful family, and we have both thrown members of our families together on a couple of occasions and that has been good. So, it is really lovely to have this history and an ongoing relationship, and I look forward to the things that are going to grow out of this work together, and to what will happen after this next phase of your life and the writing you're going to be doing then. I'm very excited about that.

Perhaps we could talk a little bit about spirituality generally before we jump into some of the more deeply theological stuff, because for me, it's significant that I've asked you on a couple of occasions to pray with me about something important, some big decision, some difficulty that my family and I are wrestling with. I know that for my own part, I am still struggling to put together a useful prayer practice after having grown up in a tradition where the prayer practice we had was largely transactional.

In the Southern Baptist Church in which I was raised, the idea was that if you were right with God, you would receive things, not necessarily the things you wanted, although that was usually how it was expressed, that God would be onboard with you and with what you were doing as opposed to the converse, which I now think I believe. And I know that you have a richly developed prayer practice, and have written several books about praying with icons. I wonder if you might talk about your prayer practice, what it is for you . . .

RW: I suppose that the difference was that I grew up, at least in my teens, in a religious environment where the worship was largely sacramental. I had a remarkable parish priest who had a richly developed prayer life. And he was steering us gently toward a more contemplative, a more receptive mode of prayer. But there was a week I went on when I was about seventeen, a week or a part of a week, for teenagers who were considering ordination in the Church, and at the retreat house I picked up a book by Christopher Butler called *Prayer* [1983]. Christopher Butler was a Benedictine monk, he was an abbot of one of the Roman Catholic monasteries in England, quite a scholar. But this was a very, very simple book.

The thing I remember from it, still, is that he said there's a difference between attention and intention. You set aside a bit of time for prayer. Your mind wanders. It doesn't seem to make much sense. Nothing much is going on. The clock ticks, and at the end of the period, you think, *Well, that wasn't much use, was it?* Well, says Abbot Butler, don't panic. If you're going down the road—this is in the very old days—to post a letter, people posted letters, you stick on the stamp, you walk down the road to the postbox. The whole of that time, your intention is posting a letter. What makes sense in that period of time is that you are posting a letter. You may not, every moment of that time as you are walking, think, *I'm going to post a letter. I'm going to post a letter.* But whatever you're doing, you're doing something that takes you somewhere and something happens. So, he says, that's a little bit like what happens in a lot of prayer. The intention is real, the attention wobbles. Don't be too surprised if that happens.

GG: Right.

RW: That was a bit of a trick moment for me. I thought, *Ah, yes.* So the attention I try to bring to prayer doesn't mean I've got to furrow my brow, concentrate furiously all the time. It means I have to be clear as I begin, this is a time given to God. And just as if I were walking down the road and suddenly veered off into a side street to buy myself a cup of coffee or whatever, I might want to think, *Hey, what am I doing? I'm supposed to be posting a letter.* So, if I find myself wandering down a side road during prayer time, I've got to say to myself, "Hey, just a minute. What am I meant to be doing here?" And gently come back onto the road. Renew my intention. Very basic. But to me, that was a breakthrough as a teenager, and helped me cope with the idea that in prayer, you have to find those disciplines of quieting your mind and your heart without huge investments of effort all the time. A way of just breathing in the grace of God. And so when I discovered, around the same time, the Eastern Orthodox tradition of the Jesus Prayer—you just repeat, "Jesus Christ, Son of God, have mercy on me, a sinner"—I thought, *Yes, that's if you like the steady one foot in front of each other going down the road to post a letter.* That's the rhythm, and that really established for me the bedrock of discipline for the rest of my life. When I think about it, I don't know that I've ever done anything very different to that in prayer.

There have been times when I realized much more intensely how much I need to be critically aware of particular kinds of distractions, particular kinds of fantasies and fugues that arise, how I need to be more self-conscious about my body and my position, the rhythm of my breath. My Buddhist friends have helped me more than I can easily say in focusing there. But it essentially remains that—a pair of basic insights. The attention wobbles, but you know where you want to go, and you try to keep yourself on the road with a set of rhythms and disciplines that just anchor you. That is it for me. I want to fix the direction, I think.

GG: I remember a friend from seminary whose spiritual director told her that the most important thing was showing up. I think for a lot of people, prayer is directed by a need in a moment. Anne Lamott talks about "help me, help me, help me" and "thank you, thank you, thank you."

RW: Help, thanks, wow.

GG: One of the things that has been really helpful for me is to think about that language of showing up. I think of it, in fact, in terms of the artistic practice that we both are familiar with. I have students who insist that they can only write when they feel inspired. And what I tell them is that you're not going to have a very successful literary career if you only write on the days when you feel that you are bursting with creativity, when you feel that you are inspired, that you are near to that Divine whatever it is. And that has sort of helped me make sense of a prayer life in which I recognize that I said I'm supposed to do this and be present and make myself present knowing that some days I'm not going to be knocked off my feet but knowing also that the chances that I'm going to make that connection and hear something that I may need to hear is that much greater because I'm there. Because I'm present. And I continue to sort of work at that. I find that like most of us, I have to get away. Retreats are really valuable for me because I spend so much time in church settings, and so I find that often I have to get out of church settings for retreats. So I'm spending the summer in a cathedral, of course . . .

RW: Like you do.

GG: But at the end of the summer I might go up to the mountains and get immersed in God in that way. Last summer I went into the mountains in New Mexico for four or five days after the summer of writing. I spent that whole trip in nature. Strangely enough, because I hadn't used it for years, I found myself praying the Trisagion over and over again ["Holy God, Holy and Mighty, Holy Immortal One, have mercy upon us"], singing it, really, as I hiked, surrounded by river and mountains. And I'm not sure exactly why that prayer, that moment, but it was clearly something I needed.

RW: Yes. I recognize what you're saying there, because even when I'm on retreat in more ecclesiastical settings—one of the places I go, of course, is a monastery on an island off the Welsh coast—what I value is not just the discipline of the monastic life, it's the cliff path early in the morning. Or, I can recall walking through the woodlands part of the island, and as you say, the insistent rhythm of walking. Insistent is not quite the right word. Steady. The steady rhythm of praise and acknowledgment. And you're simply saying, "Well, there it is. There it is." A way of saying let God's world be. And for some reason, walking in the rain. Not a very New Mexico experience. A very Welsh one. For me, that's often been a kind of very grace-filled experience, because as I've said, there is absolutely nothing you can do about rain. Just nothing at all you can do about it. It happens. You get wet. Get used to it. And the feeling of exhilarating helplessness in the face of it all. It's discovering, yes, I'm a creature, I'm a part of this created system. As in *King Lear*, "When the rain came to wet me once" [act 4, scene 6]. I can't do anything about it, and that's fine. That's fine. When you sense that, the rain becomes itself a kind of baptism of grace. To feel the moisture streaming down. You're immersed in something.

But, the just showing up thing. I think that's really important, and it's one of the things which helps us, I'd say, to challenge the Romanticism that can distort both the writing life and the praying life. The Romanticism which says that if I'm praying seriously, I ought to be having ecstatic warm feelings all the time. If I'm writing properly, I ought to be burning with creativity. And I think there of someone like Anthony Trollope, turning out his 10,000 words a day just like clockwork, just keep doing it. Or indeed, of Johann Sebastian Bach, presumably churning out cantatas week after week, and the sublime comes out just because he turns up.

The other image I've used about prayer, and maybe it applies to the writing life too, is it's a little bit like lying on a sunbed, and you put yourself where something can happen. You may not feel like anything is changing. But you're putting yourself somewhere. And in prayer you're putting yourself where the grace of God can get at you. I think it's true in some sense in the writing life as well, isn't it? You don't decide to simply say, "I'm going to spend a day writing." I might say, "I'm going to spend a day inviting the possibility of writing." By making sure certain kinds of distractions—

GG: Right.

RW: Certain kinds of pressure and busyness don't happen. And if I end up with a sentence, that's fine. I've been where something can shift in and around me.

GG: My writing practice is very much like that, because as you know, I step away for a bit from my regular life. It is a challenging thing, but as you say, it's about removing distractions. And many of those distractions are distractions we love.

RW: Of course. Or distractions we create deliberately to avoid getting down to writing.

GG: Doesn't the oven need to be cleaned?

RW: Yes.

GG: Yes, it does. I think that's a really lovely analogy, to say that not only am I going to make myself available, but I'm going to put myself in a situation where I have the most opportunity to succeed in this practice. I think the other thing is, that just like writing, the more you do prayer, the more you show up, the more those muscles . . .

RW: Are getting flexed. Yes. We say we get in tune. Muscles are getting tuned up or toned up. I've always been very struck by that particular use of words, which comes originally from the Stoics, where the *tonos* of the universe is the tuning of the universe. And an ethical life is trying to get aligned with that *tonos*. That sort of vibration of relation between things as they truly are. And as I say, whether or not you end up with a product is unpredictable, or at least I find it so. So for me I don't often get the chance to set aside a block of time for writing, but I know that if I get, say, a long plane journey, or train journey, if I don't take any very serious reading, and if I have my notebook out, I will deliberately say, "Okay, this is a time for inviting."

GG: Let me come back to Wales for a moment. That actually is one of the things we both love. You, of course, are Welsh.

RW: Indeed.

GG: You were the archbishop of Wales; you will, we expect, retire back to Wales when you are finished with this mission that you are involved in at Magdalene College, Cambridge. I have spent a number of months in Wales over the last ten years writing, and have found it to be a sacred place for me as well. I was struck as you were talking about walking in the rain about the many ways in the Celtic Christian tradition that we are with God and the saints and the angels in that outdoor setting. That resonated powerfully with me before I knew anything about Celtic Christianity or even before I ever been to Wales, because I would go someplace like New Mexico, and even when I didn't have a vocabulary for God's presence, even in some of the most difficult times in my life, I felt this sense of peace and connection, that I was in contact with something much larger than myself. I know that you have been translating a lot of Welsh of late, and I'm wondering if there are particular Welsh writers or Welsh saints with whom you feel an affinity.

RW: I've always been just a wee bit skeptical of the Celtic Christianity craze, which sometimes just wants to make Celtic Christianity a self-centered New Age thing. I don't recognize that in the literature. But I do recognize in Welsh and Irish literature, as sometimes in Anglo-Saxon literature and, indeed, in early Russian or German writing, that sense of simply being actively accompanied in the world by that utterly self-giving, sustaining energy in which the world belongs. And I think that is there in the Welsh tradition very strongly, even in some of the great Calvinist hymn writers of the eighteenth century, who in some ways would have repudiated an affirmative theology of creation, and yet discover it again in their writing. So that the writing of Williams Pantycelyn or Anne Griffiths is actually full of unexpected and luminous images that have to do with the actuality of the world. Even the very simple theme that comes again and again in Pantycelyn of being on a pilgrimage and not being able to see over the next hilltop, or being caught in a squall of rain on a hilltop as you're walking in Wales, and that's the life of discipleship. That's the life of the spirit for Pantycelyn. And the longing, the yearning, for homecoming, which is somehow not a refusal of the world we're in but a yearning to be in its center, in its very living center, which is quite different.

All of that still speaks to me, and among the great twentieth-century Welsh writers, the one who still speaks most to me is Waldo Williams, a schoolteacher, Quaker, peace activist, and saint of West Wales, of Camarthenshire and Pembrokeshire. There's something about his legacy in all those respects that to me speaks enormously powerfully. His greatest, his most famous poem "Mewn Dau Gae" ("In Two Fields" or "Between Two Fields") simply describes an experience he has joining in the haymaking on the farm, and the sense of being, as he puts it, really drawn together as if by a net. [Rowan's translation of the poem from the Welsh appears in *The Poems of Rowan Williams*, 2004.] As if some immense welling up from the earth has drawn all the workers together in a unity they can't quite understand. And that becomes for him a moment of real epiphany. He talks about a great tide of light flowing across the fields, and whenever I go to West Wales, and particularly certain bits of West Wales, around the Preseli Mountains and the wonderful spot where his memorial stands, I think of that tide of light flowing across the fields.

GG: You know that one of my favorite poems is R. S. Thomas's "The Bright Field"—[In *Laboratories of the Spirit*, 1975, and *Collected Poems: 1945–1990*, 2000]

RW: "The Bright Field." Exactly. Yes.

GG: That for me sort of encapsulates for me everything that we're talking about. That epiphany, that moment of connection and awareness in the everyday. There's nothing special about this field. But this is the field where the treasure lies.

RW: It's an unusually positive poem for R. S.

GG: It is. It is, rather.

RW: But it's fascinating that at times—and he knows he's an old curmudgeon—and he will deliberately make a poem out of the difficulty and the reluctance he has in recognizing when the light shines. So in one of the poems, "Go on, say it. Yes, all right. Yes, this is the eternal real in time, yes, this is it." And "The Bright Field" is particularly wonderful because it uses that biblical image of the treasure in the field. It's not that this is a kind of bland nature mysticism—all you have to do is be a sort of Super Wordsworth and go out and everything will be clear to you—

GG: Your eye is all that matters. Bring your eye to this place—

RW: Right. Not quite that. The sense of sheer agency calling, which at certain moments a landscape can give. Waldo Williams, again, likes to use the language of recognition. Somehow in some landscapes, in some circumstances, there's a sound, a voice, a presence, and you just recognize. This is you. This is where you belong. And he wonderfully uses in "Mewn Dau Gae" that image of the shepherd whistling for the sheepdog, and you hear that whistle at an infinite distance, but the shepherd's called.

GG: I love all of these very homely images—the master and the sheepdog, the field in the middle of nowhere, but everywhere.

RW: And you find it also in the work of somebody who wouldn't at all describe himself as a religious poet in the conventional sense, Seamus Heaney. The digging in the fields. The basic Ulster farming environment so many of Seamus's poems are about. That wonderful image of the metal scoop in the grain barrel, you can just see the gleam of the metal in it. [Seamus Heaney, "Mossbawn: Two Poems in Dedication for Mary Heaney, I. Sunlight," in *North*, 1975, and *Poems, 1965–1975*, 1980]

GG: It also makes me think—since we have moved afield from Wales to Ireland—of the *Carmina Gadelica*, the marvelous poems and prayers in that gathered sequence from the Highlands of Scotland [ed. Alexander Carmichael]. [God is with me now as I bank the fire. God is with me now as I bake the bread. God is with me now as I lead the cattle out.] Back to my question about the practice of prayer, that was tremendously influential for me. We don't just pray in those moments when we have great need. God is present in the smallest activities.

RW: And that's a theme that you find in the mainstream of Christian spirituality. You find it in Saint Teresa, you find it in the Benedictine tradition, it's something that Thomas Merton writes about from time to time. Although the word "mindfulness" has acquired a particular kind of contour these days, that's what they're writing about. In effect, Saint Teresa says that in union with God, you are able to wash the dishes more effectively. You are present in your washing of the dishes. There's a British writer called Philip Toynbee who was a very aggressive agnostic throughout his life, but in his last years, wrote a couple of spiritual journals [*Part of a Journey*, 1981, and *End of a*

Journey, 1982]. He found his way back to a religious practice, a sort of Christian religious practice, and wrote very eloquently about it. He said that one of the hardest things in the life of the spirit, as he was discovering it, was simply being present to what you were doing, and the biggest temptation for him was to be doing three things at once. So he describes feeling hungry in the middle of the night, getting up, making himself a sandwich, sitting down with the sandwich, and immediately opening a book, because you have to be doing two things at once. And what an effort it was to say, No. I am eating a sandwich. So. I am eating. Eating. Eating. And when he was digging in the garden, so, I am digging. Digging. Digging. Because, he said, maybe that will help me when I come to the time that I am dying. Dying. Dying.

GG: That's also in the Thomas poem ["The Bright Field"]. It's not the remembered past, the imagined future, straying off in either of those directions, but being present in that moment. That is an essential teaching. I certainly need to be reminded.

RW: Because it's the place where we see that spirit and body are not two things. There's an organic reality which is the body we are. That body, strangely, unpredictably, makes meanings, makes communication. It does more than it has to. But that meaning making can only ever begin when we inhabit where we are. And being settled in that sense where we are is the beginning of everything. First, arrive. Eating. Eating. Digging, Digging. And I've sometimes said to people talking about prayer or meditation, sometimes it helps to run your hand over the arm of the chair. Settle yourself onto the cushion, and feel your buttocks sinking into the cushion. Smell the carpet. Rub your hands on the carpet. Make that anchorage.

GG: Be here.

RW: Put out all those little filaments that attach you to this place. This time. Because you could say, putting it very mythologically, if God comes knocking on this particular door at this particular moment and you're not there, God may stand at the door and knock, but it may take you quite a while to arrive back from wherever fantasy world you've fled into just to open the door.

GG: That's a particularly important teaching for us just now because we distract ourselves in an infinite number of ways. In ways that our ancestors could not have imagined. I rode up to Cambridge on the train this morning, and everyone on the train was in their own little world, their own headphone-created reality. That is, more and more, the reality for the people that we want to reach. How do we talk to them about being centered and present, and not feel as though they have to be entertained and occupied. I see this in my own kids, who have been raised in this culture where they are accustomed to being occupied, rather than being entirely present.

RW: We all struggle with it. It's not just our children, is it? They've simply found new ways of being distracted. But I do wonder sometimes whether we're becoming for all our supposed materialism, a less and less physical culture. Where we don't—and I put myself in this category—we don't do the kind of physical work our parents did. And there's a liberating element in that. We don't have to do the same back-breaking kind of physical labor in the house that our grandparents and great-grandparents took completely for granted. Not all of us are gardeners, to put it mildly. I think that does make a bit of a difference. And again, one of the things that you might want to say if you were encouraging someone to explore the life of the spirit is to start by exploring the life of the body. Start with gardening. Cooking. Whatever.

Talking (name-drop alert!) with Marilynne Robinson a few months ago when we were asked in front of an audience what we thought the really substantial things were in renewing the spiritual life, we both agreed that gardening and cooking might be a place to start.

GG: Those are great places to start. I had dinner with our friends the Ditchfields last night in London [The Rev. Tim Ditchfield is head of the chaplaincy at King's College, London], and one of the things Tim and I have in common, among many, is that we both love to cook. There is this immediacy. You must be present. I have noticed that when I try to do more than something else while I'm cooking, then everything goes wrong. It's an incredible spiritual discipline.

RW: Yes, I'm not a great cook. But one of the things I do enjoy is making bread, because it takes the time it takes. I don't really approve of mechanical bread makers. I think you need to take the time for kneading and letting it rise and all the rest of it. And anything that just takes the time it takes is one of those things that hauls you in a bit. But we were also talking a bit earlier about singing, and people forget that singing is a physical activity that has some of the same centering effect. The less we sing, the worse things go. That's not going to work whistling "Heigh ho, heigh ho, it's off to work we go," it's recognizing that song is a way of inhabiting your body in a deeply affective, deeply transforming way, being and saying more than you think you are. Song together is powerful.

I was just talking to someone yesterday about a really powerful book from about ten years ago, *The Singing Neanderthals* [Stephen Mithin, 2005], which is about our remote uncles and aunts, and how the evidence suggests that Neanderthals had the capacity to sing. What we can see of their skulls, the cavities and formations around neck and throat and mouth, they probably sang rather than spoke. And speech becomes a sort of distilled, reduced form of song. So rather than song being a sort of luxury that we've invented to keep ourselves entertained, song is basic speech. It's being there for oneself, and one another, and God. Which is why we quite rightly do a lot of it in churches.

GG: Our daughter Lily is one who sings in the shower. She does not know that she is being heard, although I hear her with joy, because she is singing with joy. She doesn't necessarily sing anywhere else, but there is that very clear connection that she is making to herself and the joy she feels from doing that, and in that moment, not only is she right where she is, but anyone who hears her is right where they are, paying attention, living in that place and that moment. I mark those moments of hearing her sing as holy.

Conversation Two

In Which Rowan and Greg Discuss: Cooperation and Community / The Creative Process / Writing the Novel / Meeting Characters / Reading and Empathy / Trollope and Dickens / Marilynne Robinson / Everyone's Story Matters / Characters and Redemption / Story Endings / Sequels / Doubting Thomas / Augustine and P. D. James

GG: In our last piece of conversation, we were talking about my daughter Lily singing in the shower, and the joy that she found in that, and in her being present for herself. But the other thing I was thinking about was that last week for the first time in a while, I sang with a choir. I did the Fauré *Requiem* with the Paris Choral Society. Singing with a group is something that I've always loved. The director of the Choral Society, Zach Ullery, who is canon for music at the American Cathedral in Paris, said something that you made me think about in your talk about singing with others, which of course represents the communal and liturgical life that we have together as a church. Zach said to us, after a long, hot day of rehearsals in a stifling room, "One of the most noble things that human beings do is to come together as a community to create something beautiful." That struck me as very true, and as an essential reminder that even though we think of art as being individual and happening in a space by itself, there are also these ways that we come together and create, and singing is a really potent example of that.

RW: Yes, and also an example of what some social scientists are getting more interested in, and that is goods which are necessarily cooperative. There are some things that cannot be had except by cooperation.

GG: Right.

RW: And the choir or the orchestra is a blindingly obvious example of that. You cannot mark yourself out without ruining the entire ecology of a performance. It's like rowing a boat in a team, once again, that is a good that can only be achieved cooperatively. If you're rowing faster than everyone else, you're not actually doing the job. Because we begin from a very individualistic default setting these days, it's hard for people to get their minds around the fact that there just are these things that can only be had in this way, and perhaps when we look at our social arrangements, we might like to think about the actual social goods for human beings that can only be had cooperatively, rather than vaguely thinking, *Oh, they'll sort themselves out*. We have to be a little more intentional about that and say, there are certain aspects of our society like the care of the poor and the welcome of the stranger which are necessarily cooperative, therefore which necessarily require particular groups or individuals to step back and align with a common purpose.

GG: It is so hard for us to subsume ourselves, to step back and do that. It makes me think of this past semester at Baylor. I may have told you that I had a really challenging teaching experience where I had a student who felt like everything she wanted to say was essential to the well-being of the class, when of course the actual truth was that the well-being of the class depended on everyone being involved, everyone being heard. Ultimately I was able to explain that to her as she became more and more enmeshed in the community and, honestly, as they extended more and more grace to her as they recognized that she was trying to learn that essential skill, which is a hard skill for us.

RW: Yes.

GG: By the end of the semester, we had come to that place you recognize from your teaching where you no longer have a roomful of individuals. You have a group of people whose life together has been made possible and made better by the fact that each of them was able to step back and enable the others to become something during the course of that semester.

RW: It's a really key step forward, I think, because it's so easy to assume that if somebody says step back or step down, they're imposing something or denying something. And yet, when you're told not to let your voice drown others in a choir, it's not that you are being suppressed, it's that what is there is being allowed to emerge. It's not the director or the conductor's whim or power mania that says, "Just keep it down a bit." It's The Need, as Doris Lessing called it, what the whole global situation requires. You can't do it unless you're aware that that is the space into which you step together.

Do you know that image that Doris Lessing uses? It's in her science fiction. The Canopus in Argos series [Collected in *Canopus in Argos: Archives*, 1992]. Some of them are a bit turgid. But she wrote them because she discovered, as never before, a kind of religious dimension to her imagination, and the best way she could deal with this was through science fiction. When people there talk about the moral and the spiritual, they talk about The Need. There is something that requires—doesn't demand or bully or coerce—but requires, draws out from you The Need. That's an image I like and resonate with. I wish we could find more ways of using that sort of language. In this musical connection, The Need is the nature of the choral or orchestral work that is before you.

So should we say a few words about the practice of writing? We've touched on it already, in the way that making the space for invitation is part of what we're doing. But I wanted to ask you as a novelist a bit about how that works. It's not something I've tried my hand at all. But when I have tried writing dialogue for drama and so forth, I do have this strong sense of listening to what's unfolding, not just plucking things out of the air, but listening for where a conversation is going in my mind. Is this something as a novelist that you do?

GG: It is. For me, it's a long and very involved process. My writing practice has evolved around my teaching. As someone who takes teaching seriously—not every writer does—I want my students to have the most powerful, transformative experience they can have, and so I find that during the semester a lot of my creative energy is going into the classroom. It's going to responding to their work, it's going to creating a space where they feel heard and what they're doing well can be acknowledged and all of those things.

My first book [*Free Bird*] came out in 2002. Over the last sixteen or so years, the process that I've mostly followed—I spend a tremendous amount of time, and I think this goes back to the conversation we were having earlier about prayer—I spend a lot of time thinking, imagining, journaling, but not necessarily what most people would think about as "writing." I'll make notes, I'll write some scenes, but in terms of the actual typing, which is what most people identify as writing, I spend a couple of years with the characters, typically, before I try to put them down on paper in that way.

Every writer, of course, is different. Michael Ondaatje, who is a novelist I really admire, talks about how his process is writing a really rough discovery draft. He puts his characters on a journey and follows alongside them. As with every relationship, the longer you listen to them talking and the more you watch them in action, the more you can anticipate what they're going to do in a given situation. Of course, they'll surprise you sometimes. But my process is largely built around this long companionship with these characters.

So I do listen to them and get a sense of what they sound like. Dialogue is always built around conflict and a need. Bad dialogue is when people are talking to each other and there is nothing served by it. You get a sense during the time that you spend listening to them, whether that's in drafting or simply in sitting with them, what it is that they care about, what it is that they need, where it is in their lives that they are broken, what has got to be overcome, and the conversations that grow out of those, particularly when—as they rarely do, but they must, at some point—they begin to talk about those things that they spend most of the story not talking about.

So for me, a big, big part of that practice is showing up, over and over and over again as we were talking about showing up for God. It has worked for me because I found a way to get to that long-deferred typing stage ready to put something on the page. That has worked really well for me, although it wouldn't work for everyone, and everyone has a different process and approach. But having spent so much time letting the story gestate and listening to the characters, I usually find that when it is time to write, and I know that I have a limited time to write, whether I'm coming here to the UK or to Paris to write, I know I have this many weeks to get something on the page. It seems to flow very naturally.

I think the gestation metaphor is not a bad metaphor. You know what your due date is, so to speak, and either labor begins naturally or it is induced, and at the end of that time, there is no option other than giving birth to this thing that you have been carrying around for all this time.

The other thing that I think is really interesting about this process of writing a novel is that you come to know these characters so incredibly well, and so, as probably happened when you wrote your play, you delve into these characters, you spend time with them, you work on draft after draft, they become real to you. When I arrived in Paris last week, I went to Harry's New York Bar, where several important scenes in my new novel take place, and I will tell you that while I knew rationally that I had created a bartender in Harry's named Frederick, I was still in some ways stunned to walk in and sit down in Mr. Hemingway's chair and not see Frederick serving drinks. I had spent two years and some months getting to know him, coming to love him, and as I finish up that novel, I am in some ways bereft at the end of these relationships.

RW: Because the people disappear. Or go into another level of reality with the readership.

GG: They go on and become real for someone else. I relinquish my hold on them.

RW: I was thinking of something that appears in the introduction to one of my favorite novels, and that's *The Man on a Donkey*, by H. F. M. Prescott [1952], one of the great historical novels of the 1950s. It's about sixteenth-century England, the Reformation in England, and Hilda Prescott says in a foreword to the novel that she spent a lot of time letting readers get to know her characters as they would in real life, that is, the scenes in which we first meet them are not overdetermined, they're not necessarily contributing to the plot. You may think, *Well, why are they there?* Well, you're getting to know them. Just eavesdropping and all that.

So with one of the characters there are scenes from her childhood and her teens. The only contribution they make to the novel as such is that later on you're able to say, "I see where that comes from." And that particular instance is quite significant. One of the characters is Christabel Cowper, prioress of Marrick, head of this small, rather stodgy Benedictine convent in north Yorkshire. And if we only met her in the middle or the end of the book, we would see the woman she has become, which is a competent, hard-nosed, not insensitive, but very self-interested shrewd woman who's forgotten why she might have been a nun. But Prescott allows us to meet her first as a small girl going to the convent for the first time, and the convent school. Allows us to see her involved in an early adolescent romance with a local boy, which of course comes to nothing. Allows us to see her beginning her life in the convent. We see the steady attrition of not very easy relationships in the convent. We see her hardening inch by inch. And the result is that when we see her as a mature woman in the body of the book, there is that mixture of pity as well as distaste. With every one of the main characters we see that. I think that is the art of love in a novelist's work.

GG: It is this incredible gift we get from the great storytellers that we understand both something about those characters and something about ourselves as a result of that. We learn not to judge so harshly, and I hope we carry that over from novels, from plays, from movies into our own lives. I tend to write about characters who are very badly broken by their pasts, so something like this prioress, who we would not judge so harshly knowing what she's experienced. It was not in one of the novels, but I think it was actually in *Crossing Myself*, the memoir about depression, that I talked about one of the insights I got from my own suffering, which was the secret heartbreak that many, many people carry around with them of which we are not aware. Often we judge people based on outward behavior. Just to imagine loving them as God loves them, knowing them is the gift that a novelist gives us in a really well-told story. It's the gift that, as we said, we hope will transfer into our lives, where we can treat others with a little more grace.

RW: Yes. I was really struck, years ago, when I came across John Bayley's book *The Characters of Love* [1960], which is about, as he sees it, the essential requirement for a novelist, the love for characters. For him unsurprisingly, Tolstoy is the great example of that. Even with Tolstoy's most shallow or treacherous or unattractive characters, you are allowed those moments when you can see just a little bit of how and why, and even somebody like Trollope, you don't normally think of Trollope in this light, less attractive, less principled characters. He will allow you inside.

Lopez, in *The Prime Minister* [1876], who's a profoundly unattractive figure, an adventurer, unscrupulous, greedy, and ambitious, makes an unsuitable marriage to a woman who loves him for what he really isn't. He's elected to Parliament, and that's a bit of a disaster, and he eventually commits suicide. (Spoiler alert.) But Trollope gives you enough time with Lopez to think, *God, what a shame.* Because you see his self-hatred, you see his confused emotion. He's quite good at that mixture of muddle and confusion, inner violence and violence. Violence directed outside turning into violence directed inside. Several of his characters work like that, and again, some of his very unprincipled characters who are, in less dramatic ways, fraudulent about money and so forth, even there we have a little glimpse of someone just successfully milked a gullible friend for more money.

Then you see him turning away to stifle a sob in his room afterward, saying, "I've done it again." So that's love. That's love.

I think I'm inclined to agree with Bayley that you measure the greatness and the depth of a novelist by how pervasive that is and how deep it goes. And I guess Dickens gives you real villains into whose insides you have little insight, but because, I think, of the love he pours out on his major characters, you can cut him some slack on that. It's what finally, I think, makes Dickens a greater novelist than Trollope. Trollope is more universal in his sympathy, but you sometimes feel it's a bit undemanding. Dickens passionately loves the characters he loves. And you sort of allow him to hate the ones he hates as well. But even there, famously with a villain like Fagin in *Oliver Twist* [1838], you see him in prison awaiting his death sentence, and it is harrowing.

GG: We were talking about Marilynne Robinson earlier, who is a writer that we both admire, and someone who exhibits that love toward a number of characters, which has been manifested in this really startling way as she's written individual novels from the viewpoint of several characters that we were introduced to in *Gilead*. That is an incredible task that she has set for herself, to say, "This is where my story started, but every human life has a compelling story attached to it," which is the novelist's belief. And if I plucked this character out of the novel, I could tell an amazing story about her, and where she came from, and who she is now, and what has to happen in her life for her to be fulfilled or for her to be whole.

When we look at *Home* [2008], the sequel to *Gilead*, we have a character who in *Gilead* doesn't appear in her best light as a particularly sympathetic human being, and yet, when we're presented with her life. . . . And in *Lila* [2014], the third book, we've got a character who previously we've seen largely from the outside, through the consciousness of her aging husband in *Gilead*. She is doing this radical act—and you told me that Robinson is working on a fourth novel! There is something really amazing about this. There is not much like this in contemporary fiction where someone is generating this universe of characters in this tiny, tiny place and telling compelling stories about each of them. We have traditions where people will take a setting and explore characters in that setting, the Modernists, the Victorians, but there are not many writers doing that in the present.

RW: And doing it, as you say, with the awareness that each character could be the hero of a novel. Therefore the world does not divide into people with interesting lives and people with boring lives. But that the world is a world of stories, and each person has some right—some dignity—as the subject of a narrative. I think that's a really important imaginative/social/political/religious insight. I think that's why Marilynne Robinson's novels do strike so deep a chord. You know, there are novelists who will reuse characters from other books, or give you other perspective, perhaps unexpectedly, on a story by shifting the narrative circumstance, but as you say, to stick with that little group of characters and to slowly, steadily, move you around from one point of view to another. That's a very impressive achievement.

GG: Some years ago, I wrote a long short story ["Bridges," published in *The Long Story* in 1999] that grew out of the novel *Shame* [2009], about a character who is for me a really compelling character who spends much of his life in prison, Philip One Horse.

RW: I remember.

GG: Philip is a person who's brought into the story as a sort of—rescue project is a very literal way of thinking about his role in the novel—but partly it grows out of John, the main character in *Shame*'s awareness that they were not the friends to him that they could have been, and it's an attempt to sort of make up for that failure on their part, that they extend love and friendship to him. Philip finds it very hard to accept. In *Shame*, we see this entirely from John's point of view. But it came to me that Philip was a character with an amazing inner life. As we said, if every human has a compelling story, it means that there is a reason for who they are and why they've done what they've done and what they've become. What often happens for storytellers is you step backward and you reason backward from the brokenness or the present circumstances where you find somebody, and you ask yourself—

RW: "Where did this come from?"

GG: Why is somebody like this? As you said, this is a really important political/social/cultural/religious question to ask ourselves in terms of the validity of every human being to have their story recognized, honored. It has a ton of political implications, because in both of our countries right now we have politicians who are treating entire classes of people as though their stories don't matter. What the novelist or the great playwright or the great screenwriter tells us is that there is no human life that doesn't have dignity, no human life that is not interesting and compelling, no human life that doesn't have reasons for where it's wound up.

RW: And that doesn't suspend your judgment indefinitely, doesn't say that there are no ethical questions to be asked about peoples' decisions, which is the sort of glib response to this. But it does at least tell you that what you are judging, what you are engaging with, has a history. As long as you go on asking yourself that question, "What is the history? How did we get to this?" you're delivered from that delusory timelessness, people are just good or bad, and that's all you need to know. And it's that impatience with the process of soul-making that I think is really bad for us politically, imaginatively, morally, and religiously.

GG: There's a film that I've been teaching over the last two years, Kenneth Lonergan's *Manchester by the Sea* [2016]. It's an incredibly novelistic film. Unlike most movies, we've got a lot of interior access to its major character, Lee Chandler [Casey Affleck], who is badly broken. It's a story that treats him with incredible seriousness. So the way that that movie works is that it is actually about why this character is the way he is. He's introduced to us early on as a character who is profoundly sad, broken, taciturn, and in some ways the movie, at least the first half of it, is a mystery that gets resolved for us about halfway through when we have a long flashback and we discover that he's lost his entire family as a result of a mistake that he made.

It is this incredibly powerful film, and as you said, it doesn't mean that we suspend judgment. Because one of the responses that people have to the end of the film is that they don't think that Lee has gone anywhere. Kenneth Lonergan talked about the movie at the Austin Film Festival, and he said, "I don't write stories in which people end up in precisely the same place where they began." But if we think of a character's arc as being A to Z, in its broadest outlines, then this is a character who goes from A to D. And we can see these tiny little pieces of progress, of *metanoia*, but it's not full redemption, and he's still tremendously broken. But that's also a true story.

RW: Very much so. I think that's one of the strengths of Dostoevsky's *Crime and Punishment* [1866]. That at the end, Raskolnikov has not actually turned into a nice person. He is sort of repentant, but not very. He's a work in progress. And I think Dostoevsky trusts us to say, "Do we trust this story to be going somewhere?" Rather than giving us the resolution we long for. And that's a risk, and it's interesting when novelists take that risk. I was thinking of that the other day because I was watching a dramatized version of *Great Expectations* [1861] in the theatre. A difficult novel to stage. And I was wondering, *Which version of the ending are they going to go for? Dickens's original unresolved, or the happy ending that was finally imposed on him?* They found a very neat way of not resolving that which was perfectly okay.

But of course Dickens in his first draft was saying something really, really interesting. He was saying, "Having set this up with these characters, this is where they're going to end up. Anything else is going to break the whole integrity of what I've been writing." It's not a hopeless ending. But it's not a happy ending. And again, you have to trust that where Pip has got to at the end of the book, and where Estella has got to by the end of the book, that's where they get to, because that's who they are. And he's not going to interfere with that. As I say, it's not hopeless, but it's certainly not easy, and generation after generation has wanted the happy ending.

GG: Right.

RW: And yet as Dickens knew perfectly well, he would have to do real violence to both his main characters—especially to Estella—so, respect to Dickens for taking the risk.

GG: One of my favorite novels is Hemingway's *The Sun Also Rises* [1926]. We have these two characters we would dearly love to see together, even though they would probably be terrible for each other. Hemingway's approach to the end of the novel is to say it would be nice if this could happen. But it can't. "Wouldn't it be lovely to think so?" is Jake Barnes's response to the idea of the proffered happy ending. That's a very human ending, because a lot of times, our stories don't end with a 180-degree turn, that *metanoia* that we talk about as the spiritual goal.

RW: But to believe that these stories are, in some sense, infused with grace, doesn't mean that you've got to get everybody married with two kids, as it were, in the last chapter. It simply means that you've got to demonstrate, within the integrity of the characters that you've created, a reality of change, or grace, or whatever.

GG: Those are happy endings.

RW: With your novels, there is resolution of some sort at the end. But I wouldn't say that they go all out for happy endings. As if you could draw a line and say, "And they lived happily ever after." That's finished business. There's still work to do.

GG: I think in some ways they are theologically accurate, although I didn't set out to write them as theological documents. They represent that understanding of grace and the possibilities that come with that understanding. One of my teachers at the University of Iowa, the Pulitzer Prize–winner Robert Olen Butler, used to say to us, "If you're going to be a god, be a merciful god." And what I think he meant by that is that, as opposed to, let's say, some of the naturalist writers like [Stephen] Crane or [Theodore] Dreiser, who would basically say, your life is going to end unhappily, no matter what you choose, because that's just the nature of the universe. As you're sitting here and thinking about whether you should steal the money out of that safe, the door is somehow going to slam shut, and you are going to be prohibited from making a choice [Dreiser, *Sister Carrie*, 1900]. What I think that Butler was trying to get us to do as novelists was to make every possibility open for our characters. And particularly that possibility of grace that would allow them to possibly escape from the reality of their tortured lives, because really the best novels are about people who have tortured lives.

RW: The only qualification I'd put, I think, is to use the word "escape," not as if it's a leap over the wall, but there is a path here, there is a way. Not just slipping out from under. And that's where I think the escape, if you want to call it that, has to be earned, so whatever resolution or opening possibility that occurs arises from where you've been. The possible arises from the actual, to use an Aristotelian phrase.

GG: In each of my four novels, and this fifth one that I'm finishing now, I think you're right to say that we don't have that 180-degree turn that we hope for when we see someone who has amended their life and their way of being. It's not a Dickensian I'm going to tell you what happened to these characters several years or generations down the road. I think actually the best way to think about it is to look at the main character, Brad Cannon, at the end of my second novel, *Cycling* [2003]. He has had this really difficult life, and he's experienced terrifying heartbreak, and his reaction to that is to try not to live. His yearning, so to speak, is not a positive yearning—I want to accomplish this—but a negative yearning—I don't want to be hurt anymore. And of course we realize that this is not accurate to the human condition. You can't—short of stepping off the planet—there is no way of removing yourself from that very real possibility of heartbreak, which becomes more intensely painful the more you care.

What that character needs most is to take that tiny step in which he says, "I can think about beginning to live again." A character in their final conversation in the book actually uses the word "grace." And again, I was not a particularly religious person when I wrote that novel, but there are so many true theological stories, so many human stories, that he is talking about—in the same way that Hemingway talked about "Wouldn't it be lovely to think so?"—a step beyond that.

RW: Yes. A step beyond that.

GG: To say, "I want to think so." When he is introduced to that concept of grace, that idea that you haven't earned this, you haven't merited it, but all the same it is offered to you. This possibility. This wondrous possibility. And for him to say, "I want to seize that." And we don't see where he goes with it. That's where the curtain comes down.

RW: But the wanting itself becomes a factor. It's a new factor in the overall situation.

GG: So just as with Pip and Estella, this is where the story ends. And to go on from here is a new story. I've actually thought sometimes about writing a sequel to *Cycling*, which was my absolute worst-selling book. No one else is interested in that project. But Walker Percy and Richard Ford, who are two of my great literary heroes, have come back to characters they loved.

RW: Indeed.

GG: And written sequels concerning them.

RW: *The Second Coming* [1980], isn't it? Picking up from *The Last Gentleman* [1966]?

GG: And Richard Ford's series about Frank Bascombe, who he wrote about first in *The Sportswriter* [1986]. *The Sportswriter* was intended as a sort of homage to Walker Percy's *The Moviegoer* [1961]. And my *Cycling*'s original title was *The Cyclist*, but my publisher didn't think that anyone would care about the literary allusion, and then they went on to put an action/adventure cycling photo on the cover so that it was misfiled by Barnes & Noble in the Sports section.

RW: Not what you want.

GG: No. It wasn't. But that is a character I loved so dearly and rooted for so hard. And honestly did not know until the end of my story if he was going to accept that dangled grace. Which is sometimes the way. In some of the stories, I've had a very clear sense what direction the grace was going to carry the characters, sometimes down to the actual language. Endings are essential, and they are tied to the beginning so that in in some way you have come back full circle, you've translated an entire journey. With Brad, that character in *Cycling*, I was literally rooting for him the entire time I was writing, to see some sort of light. That was all he was capable of at that point, but I believe that having turned even slightly in that direction, an entire new life becomes possible for him. And I would love to know what that life was. I may be the only person who wants to know.

RW: But it is a telling way of putting it, isn't it? I would love to know what that life was? It's a witness to that element of writing which is discovery rather than invention. You have to go back and do the hard work of saying, "Having come to this point, where is the next natural phase in that pattern?"

GG: And you know our sacred stories are full of so many of those things. Because I don't serve in a church full-time, I find that I'm often invited to come and preach Easter II.

RW: Rector's holiday, yes.

GG: I am preaching Doubting Thomas yet again. But you know we have this apocryphal story about Thomas, who turns a corner, who accepts that dangled grace, and who becomes a martyr in this far-off land [India]. There is this whole story that comes after the Gospel lesson that we read for Easter II. That moment of "My Lord and My God, I see you," I can do something with that. That's the real-life question. What comes next? Once novels suggest that we might see the world in a different way, ourselves in a different way, what do we do with that? How do we honor that moment of movement or decision? Where does it take us?

RW: Absolutely. Interesting that you should use the example of Thomas there. One of the things that is remarkable about the stories, as the evangelists record them, is character does actually matter. You get a sense of the three-dimensionality of the people around Jesus. There's a genuinely novelistic quality to the Gospels, by which I don't mean they're fiction, but novelistic in telling a story so that you can see how things follow. So, Thomas, who only appears on two other occasions in the fourth Gospel, is a consistent figure. He says in chapter 11, "Let us also go, that we may die with him" [John 11:16, NRSV] and he says later on, "We do not know where you are going. How can we know the way?" [John 14:5, NRSV]. And there are these little touches flecked in, this is somebody whose default setting is half empty.

GG: Yes.

RW: That's simply a minor example of what you have much more markedly in the depiction of Peter. Or indeed, of the Sons of Zebedee in the Gospels. You know that Peter is the person who will rush in tactlessly, sometimes getting it magnificently right and sometimes getting it disastrously wrong. You know that the Sons of Zebedee have a short fuse. You get that sense that if you like the relationships in which the Incarnate Word of God is involved, they are actual relationships. He's not a figure detached from the complexity of human relationship. He engages with—transfiguringly engages with—genuinely diverse, genuinely complex, genuinely fallible figures, and that's why I think the Gospels remain so intensely readable for a novel-reading generation.

GG: They are so well drawn that we have this sense of understanding them—as we were talking about with characters. We think we know what they are going to do. Most of the time. And then they surprise us.

RW: Yes. They surprise us.

GG: As human beings do. Because we are ridiculously capricious.

RW: But when they surprise us, we can look back and say, "Ah, yes. But I see where that comes from." So that with Thomas, yes, you've got the depressive response he makes later on. But you've also got the doggedness—sheer fidelity—even in failure. And you can say, that's what makes him ask, and that's what makes him recognize the answer. Because—and this is a condensed sermon, if you like—it's as if he sees the marks in Jesus's hands and side as if he says, "Here is somebody who has been faithful in failure, as I have been rigidly faithful in failure. Yes, I see." Something profound in him comes alive in that moment.

GG: The first time we came together we talked about novelists, and found some common favorites. You may not remember this, but I do. We were talking about the British mystery writer P. D. James, who is one of my favorite novelists, not just as a mystery writer, but as a writer. The characters she creates are full and beautifully drawn, and often they're presented in these moments where grace or transcendence or something can happen. The character of Kate, in *A Taste for Murder* [1986], who toward the end of that novel is being held hostage along—

RW: Yes, with her grandmother.

GG: Who raised her, and with whom she had this fraught, difficult relationship. And even though it doesn't end as we hoped that it would, it ends with this incredible beauty, with this movement, and this grace. I wonder if you remember that you told me that you thought of P. D. James as the great Augustinian novelist—

RW: Augustinian. I do remember, yes.

GG: I was very interested in Augustine then, this was during seminary, of course, which was my formal introduction to theology. Just as I had a very different response to Calvin than I expected to have, based on my many years of not particularly liking Calvinists, I had a very different response to Augustine, who became, present company excluded, my favorite theologian. I wonder what you meant by calling her Neo-Augustinian.

RW: It's a phrase I have used once or twice about her, because I feel that she's got a sensibility and an imagination that I want to describe as Augustinian, in the sense that even her good characters are flawed and vulnerable, and even her evil characters are pitiable and unhappy. That sounds as if Augustine is just out to put people on an equally unhappy footing of misery, but it's sort of a grown-up imagination. This will not be a story about heroes and villains. Or even, in a sense, about saints and sinners. This is going to be a story about people whose suffering and whose choices have brought them to certain places. And within those places, they still have choices. They still have freedom. They can draw closer; they can draw further away.

You can't say that they all save themselves by those choices, but the overall climate of P. D. James's fictions is, I think, enormously compassionate, and compassionate in a way that a lot of readers don't find comfortable because there are proud and difficult figures who are unlikeable, there are driven and selfish figures, superficial and shallow figures, and yet they're all seen with a sense of everyone's involvement in the collaborative unhappiness of the human race. But seen in such a way that you don't just believe that's just a death sentence. It's all complex—

GG: No, that's very nicely put.

RW: It's very hard to crystallize, but I think the example that you choose from *A Taste for Death* is a very, very interesting one, because that is certainly—that conclusion—is a moment where Kate discovers in herself an instinct for love, which has been denied and frustrated. And it's that desperate, I-can't-help-myself kind of love which brings with it no guarantees of success or, again, promise of happy endings. But it's a moment structurally a bit like *King Lear*, where Shakespeare gives us a moment of transcendent reconciliation.

GG: That's a really good analogy.

RW: But then he says, "But that's not going to save their lives, necessarily." As I've sometimes put it with *King Lear,* Shakespeare sort of stares at us from the stage and says, "That was lovely wasn't it? Now I'm going to kill them. Is that okay with you?" Is that still going to be worthwhile? Is that still going to mean something? That moment in *A Taste for Murder* of reconciliation, that moment when Kate's heart goes out to this wretched old lady who has been such a nuisance to her, such a difficult unsympathetic figure. And yet her heart goes out and P. D. James says it, like Shakespeare, "So does that matter even if it's not going to be a happy ending?" And our Augustinian answer has to be, "Yes, of course." Because we know that what happens has to be, if you like, part of the logic of the finite world we inhabit. But the miracle is that the logic of the finite world we inhabit does not actually obstruct grace.

Conversation Three

In Which Rowan and Greg Discuss: Why Shakespeare Matters / Live Drama / The Preaching Event / The Danger of the Live Event / Shakespeare on the Theatrical / Shakespeare on Politics and Power / Writing Plays / The Unity of Creative and Theological Writing / Good and Bad Christian Writing / Writing Redemption / Story and Embodiment / Literature as Theology

GG: One of the topics that has come up in every conversation we have ever had is Shakespeare. I know that you love reading the plays, talking about them, seeing them. Almost every time I see you, you have recently come from another performance. So it's clear to me that—in the way that we form our own canonical texts, our own personal interior bookshelves—many of these works are things you come back to again and again as a way of understanding the world and yourself. What makes Shakespeare so powerful for you?

RW: The first thing, I think, is just that sense of the real in Shakespeare's plays, even when dealing with fantastical, unrealistic plots. It's the sense of someone who sits very, very close indeed to the throb of ordinary human emotion—pain and anxiety and exhilaration and delusion—all of that. The sheer range of feeling that he encompasses, and the sense he conveys of having really inhabited it. I don't mean in a cheap autobiographical sense, but in his imagination inhabited the pulse and the rhythm of all these feelings. There's a sense of reality.

And then, he's a very good poet, isn't he? To state the bleeding obvious. The language continues to compel. There are scenes, there are lines, where something so completely unexpected takes over, something so beautiful in an utterly unconventional way. To me, Leontes's words at the end of *The Winter's Tale,* "Oh, she's warm" [act 5, scene 3]. The volumes of feeling beneath that. And that is one of Shakespeare's great strengths. He can, in just a couple of words, give you that intensity of feeling. Beauty is part of it, but it's not all of it. I think it was G. K. Chesterton who said that only Shakespeare could make "Undo this button" a line that broke your heart [*King Lear,* act 5, scene 3].

And then along with that, the lyricism that just carries you along. The beautiful, flawless sonnet that Romeo and Juliet exchange in their first encounter. "If I profane with my unworthiest hand" [act 1, scene 5]. That spontaneous exchange of poetry between the two. Absolutely wonderful. And the way that in *Macbeth,* which is a very verbally dense play, he can use something like "Light thickens, and the crow / Makes wing to th' rooky wood" [act 3, scene 2]. Or "And pity, like a naked newborn babe, Striding the blast . . ." [act 1, scene 5]. He can rub your nose in the grime, in the muck of evil and pain just by those images. All of that and lots more.

GG: One of the things that I've always told my students is that you can read Shakespeare. You can experience the beautiful poetry. You can do a technical study of the literary devices. You can scan the lines, you can do all the things that the text allows us to do. But the plays come to life, the characters come to life, in performance. You've seen I don't know how many performances of many of these plays. Something happens in live theatre that is a transcendent moment. I know we want to talk about pop culture later, and there's a similar thing with going to see a film, which has its own sacramental quality because of the way it tells its stories in front of an audience. But what is different about seeing a really good performance of Shakespeare as opposed to simply reading it?

RW: You become aware of the physicality of the drama. You become aware of words as a physical thing. Drama is a physical event. You've got to be there. It's nice to watch a broadcast of Shakespeare on television or one of those live-streamed productions from the Globe or the National, but actually the real experience is physically to share the space in which a kind of liturgy is being performed. Just as you can't fully take part in a liturgy just on television. So the live performance says to the audience, "We understand that you are there as a physical participant. A silent physical participant in this. Your uncomfortable lower back or aching bottom is part of what we're aware of. This is a time we share together. It will take this amount of time to get us through. There's no fast-forward button. And the words we as actors engage, we promise to speak in a way which we trust will hold you there, alert but still silent through this experience that we're sharing." And there's something rather electrifying about that promise from the stage. We will engage to keep you there, hold you as best we can, and rather like the end of *Midsummer Night's Dream* [act 5, scene 1], where Puck comes forward in a sort of half apology—

GG: "If we shadows have offended"—

RW: This may or may not have worked, but we've done our best. Bear with us. I think that's why the way in which the Globe [Theatre] company have revived the practice of having a dance at the end of every performance, even a tragedy, is quite significant. It says, now let's celebrate the fact that we have actually managed to stay in this space together for two or three hours to learn something together. Again, the physicality comes through. If you think of drama as fundamentally a physical, material change, a liturgical moment, a moment in time, that's why live performance matters.

GG: It strikes me that it's similar to other things that are events. We talk about the preaching event. I can read one of your sermons, or one of Barbara Brown Taylor's sermons, and admire them. But they don't exist in the same way. They were created in a moment, for a moment, and they will never be the same for any other audience.

RW: That's why I'm not actually wildly keen on publishing sermons. People ask for them occasionally and I've given way, and of course some of the great theology of ages past has been done in sermons. I accept that. But for me there is something a little bit inadequate about that, since a sermon is crafted for these people in this time in exactly the same way that no two performances of a play are the same.

GG: It also strikes me that there may be a—"danger" may not be the precise word—but live performance—

RW: Things can go wrong.

GG: And do. In the same way the live television has a certain excitement to it, because we don't get to practice it until we get it right. We're going to do it, as you say, the best we can, the best we are capable of in this moment. Our intention is good.

RW: Another of the fascinating features about Shakespeare is his willingness to reflect on theatre. His drama is often drama about drama. *Midsummer Night's Dream* is the archetypal comic reflection on that, and the wonderful arguments that the mechanicals have about their play, and are they going to upset people by being too realistic [act 3, scene 1]? Shouldn't someone explain that this is only a story, and so on.

Then of course in *Hamlet*, the engagement that Hamlet has with the players. But also the fact, that people often forget, that *The Taming of the Shrew* is framed as a play within a play. The imagery of the player returns in a number of dramas, not least in *Macbeth*, "A poor player / That struts and frets his hour on the stage / And then is heard no more" [act 5, scene 5]. So Shakespeare certainly sees his drama as a way of reflecting on the strangeness of drama. What is it that makes us engage in this sort of event? What is it that persuades us to sit in silence and suspend our agency and our speech so that we can be informed by this story? Well, Shakespeare says, it is pretty strange. But let's just watch how it works.

Again, Hamlet reflecting on theatrical emotion: "What's Hecuba to him, or he to Hecuba / That he should weep for her?" [act 2, scene 2]. But *Hamlet* is a sort of Mobius strip, the endless continuum.

Hamlet is saying to the audience, "Look at the nature of theatrical emotion. It's confected. It's fictitious. But that doesn't mean it's unreal. Here is somebody shedding real tears for a fictional figure. And therefore, you, the audience, are invited also. I, Hamlet, am a fictitious character. And your emotions are real." Shakespeare just gives this hall of mirrors all the time in his drama. All good drama does some of this, but Shakespeare particularly. Appearance and reality, illusion and truth, and finding truth through multiple illusion, disguise as a means of discovery—he loves all this. Really wallows in it.

GG: We were speaking earlier about this significant new book by Stephen Greenblatt, *Tyrant* [2018], which talks about the political dimension of Shakespeare. For 400 years we have found social truth, cultural truth, psychological truth, even religious truth, some theological understanding of ourselves in the plays of Shakespeare. And yet as you were saying to me earlier, we don't have this sort of autobiographical dimension to him because we just don't know that much about him.

RW: It's wonderful, in a way, that we know so little about him. The sense of a rather shadowy figure smiling enigmatically in the background of a much more vigorous and active picture. Somebody slipping just out of focus. You turn to talk to him and he's gone off somewhere else. And what we do know of him rather wonderfully suggests that he was an extremely canny businessman, that he was quite prepared, like other Tudor and Stuart people, to go to law at the least provocation to defend his possessions, and that while he was writing with heartbreaking perception about the evils of hoarding grain in times of scarcity in *Coriolanus*, he was busy doing that. He doesn't have to be a saint to be a genius.

But the political side of it is fascinating because at a time when it was quite easy for writers to fall into one of two distorted approaches to that, he really cleaves to a unique line. You could, in that time, either be a simple propagandist, or you could vote for the regime. Or you could step aside from politics and write what they called "citizen comedies" [also known as "city comedies"], soap opera of the day. Jolly stories about London merchants having adulterous affairs and impecunious apprentices having a rough night out. Shakespeare doesn't do either of those. He makes you think about how power works, again and again. And, of course, he cuts his teeth on a long series of, probably collaborative, plays on political history, the Henry VI series. And you can see him as that goes on and evolves into *Richard III*, you can see him maturing his sense of how political evil gets a grip on a society. Stephen Greenblatt is superb on this, how the description of the beginning of the War of the Roses in Henry VI shows you in a single scene how you move from a debate about something to a standoff where it no longer matters what you're disagreeing about, because the object of your disagreement has completely given way to the fact that you now know who you are because you're not them [*Henry VI, Part I*, act 2, scene 4]. And that's the moment when the genuinely political disappears. And you're on the route to civil war.

GG: And we of course live in a time of Us and Them that Shakespeare captures so well for us. One of the things we hope when we encounter narrative, whether it's a play or in a story or a film, is that if we thoughtfully interrogate it, we can see something, and perhaps see it in a way that we're incapable of seeing in our everyday life. I want to talk more about this later, because you know that I have this passion for narrative, and popular culture have filled this spiritual need for many people and have helped them to understand things, but Shakespeare does have that incredible gift of—even though we're 400 years removed—we're not at all removed.

RW: No, we're not. And that is, I think, a function of the fact that he refuses to write merely contemporary drama. He goes behind the symptoms of the political ills of the sixteenth and seventeenth centuries and encourages us to think, *How do political diseases work? What's the actual epidemiology of political decay, and where are the real risks of power and the costs of power?* And again, pursuing the history, as you move from *Richard II* to *Henry IV, Part 1*, there you see a particular model of power—Richard the Second, as a sort of God-king, arbitrary but sacred, brilliant, coruscating, and rather emotionally illiterate. We see all that swept aside by the would-be realist Bolingbroke, and you see Bolingbroke, in turn, being pushed into a corner by his own power. Again, Greenblatt brings this out very nicely. Finally he's driven, as it were, to say, meaningfully, "Wouldn't it be nice if Richard the Second were dead?" And of course, it's deniable. But when we meet him again in the Henry IV plays, he's crushed by guilt, by failure, by the fact that everything he set out to do is crumbling, by the fact that his son is alienated from him, and he's a wretched, miserable, lonely man.

Then comes the new regime, Henry V, announced with trumpets and guns, and Henry V is off to France in the play, and then we see him on the eve of battle. A very bold scene this, wandering among the soldiers, trying to get them to tell him that it's all right, and they won't. Shakespeare is merciless. He has Henry thinking, *Well, is it all right for me to be here? Do I have a claim to the throne, do I have a claim to France?* [act 4, scene 1]. *Do I have right on my side?* And you have that really chilling conversation with the soldiers at the campfire, and the soldiers will not give in. "I am afeard there are few die well that die in a battle." We have to do what we have to do, but I wouldn't want to be in the king's shoes.

GG: It's on the king.

RW: Then Henry makes that great speech "Upon the king," and it's both noble and petulant. He's both saying, "Yes, the king carries all these things," and, "For God's sake, why does everyone expect me to be responsible?" And then his prayer at the end, promising that he will build yet more chantries in memory of Richard II, and Shakespeare sort of leaves him there. Does his usual sidelong glance at the audience, saying, "Hmm." And again, the ambivalence of power is just dropped before you.

And then I mentioned that Henry VI / Richard III sequence earlier on. You've got the same scratching away at the sores, the misuse of power in a different form. It rears its head in play after play. Domestically as well as politically. *Midsummer Night's Dream*, which we think of as a nice sunny play, begins of course with the horrific dilemma that Egeus poses to Theseus [act 1, scene 1]. He is actually licensed to kill his daughter if she doesn't marry the person he wants her to marry. And patriarchy is there suddenly in its most bloodthirsty uncompromising form. We rush past that, but that's the world in which this play is happening. So again, Shakespeare is making *Midsummer Night's Dream* a play about power. Oberon's power over Titania, finally brutally reasserted by the fantasy he imposes on her. Not a pretty story. And the humiliating stories that are imposed on the human lovers. One of the most interesting moments in that play is when they all wake up in the morning and nobody's quite sure what's gone on and now they've got to make sense of it all.

The comedies are genuinely funny, wonderfully enriching and life-enhancing, but they don't spare you the underlying bleakness sometimes. *Twelfth Night*, my favorite example of a tragicomedy, achingly funny, until you realize that at the center of the humor is a terrific bit of bullying and humiliation. Not resolved at the end. So when I talk about Shakespeare's sense of reality, he will make you laugh, and he will not let you forget.

GG: You wrote a short play [*Shakeshaft*, 2016] in which you tried to enter into Shakespeare's life—

RW: God forgive me.

GG: No. It's a lovely play, it's been produced, and I think it's very fine. I had the privilege of reading an early draft of it. You took some speculation about what sort of life Shakespeare might have had, and we were talking earlier about how we want to know how characters became themselves. The question you ask in that play, essentially, is "How does he become Will Shakespeare?" We are, among other things, people who have found religion important in helping to explain who we are and where we come from. Was that a satisfying experience? Imagining the world of this playwright that you love so much?

RW: The short answer is, "Yes." Satisfying sounds a bit too smug, I suppose, but an experience that I found very enriching, just trying to imagine from the lower foothills what an imaginative life like that might have by way of connection with a complex religious background. Just as a sort of datum for the play, I took the theory that he was from a Catholic household, that he was working in a Catholic household in Lancashire. A Jesuit martyr, Edmund Campion, was resident there and it made—I'm agnostic about the historic foundation of this, but it made a certain kind of sense to suppose a young Shakespeare might have retained from his Catholic milieu at least two things. A very, very powerful sense of loss of a world that had been crumpled and torn as a result of the Reformation, so that he was already, not looking back nostalgically, but thinking, *How do you live in the aftermath of a process that has torn up the symbolic language people share? How do you begin to put the world back together again?* That's why I think that he himself must have thought of theatre as liturgical in some way.

And the second thing I was taking from that was that he must also as a Catholic moving from one safe house to another, being aware that the sixteenth-century equivalent of the state security were tracking everybody, he would have had a sense of the gaps between appearance and reality, the need for concealment of what mattered most, the way in which there were some things that could only be spoken in the most intimate possible environment, and even then you weren't quite sure who you were talking to. I think that's not a bad preparation for a dramatist, who is working all the time with misdirections and mistaken identities, secrets and so forth.

At the end of his life, when he's writing *Cymbeline*, he can be almost light-hearted about that. *Cymbeline* is full of secrets that are then revealed one by one. I think somebody said there are thirty-seven disclosures in the last scene of *Cymbeline*, and most audiences end up laughing at the succession of completely unlikely secrets that are suddenly trotted out, as if Shakespeare is saying, looking back at his whole work, it's all been about secrets and concealment and revelation and there's no point in my making it a secret any longer. Here, in the most blatant and unapologetic theatrical form, is how I do my plays.

And at the same time, I would say that gives him a very odd, very distinctive religious flavor. He's not a confessional playwright, whatever he was in his old life. He was not a practicing Catholic. He must have left that behind. We do know he was an entirely unenthusiastic member of the Church of England the rest of his life, but he's aware of something around the anarchy of grace, the terrifying surprise of forgiveness, the way in which you have to get beyond cause and effect and debt and payment. I've argued about *King Lear* that in one way, it's a play about how you move from a debt and payment economy to an economy of pure gift.

GG: Have you been working on another play? Is that something you'd want to do again?

RW: I am working on another one, actually. One of my heroes is David Jones, the Anglo-Welsh poet and artist, and he spent some time in his early life living with [sculptor] Eric Gill and was engaged to Gill's daughter, Petra. Because we now know that Gill was a serial abuser of his daughters, someone with a very complicated personal life, I find myself wondering several things about this. What, if anything, did Jones know about that, and how did that affect his artistic relationship with Gill? I don't know that he knew explicitly, but I think he must have known something at some level. That something was amiss. How did his own traumas in the First World War, a hideous experience in the War, play into his rather disastrous emotional life? How did all of that move into the miracle of his World War One poem *In Parenthesis* [1937]?

I'm still feeling my way with all that, but bits and pieces are coming together.

GG: People sometimes ask me if I see the different parts of my writing life as separate or conjoined, and as someone who also does creative work and writes theology, I want to hear what you think. I always say that I don't see a distinction, because the creative work that I'm doing is also examining who God is and who human beings are. It's doing it in a different way, of course. You were saying earlier that art is not theological in that it formulates. I find that when I'm writing a story, I'm asking a question or presenting an option. As a theologian, I'm trying to cage something, but in good art, you can't cage the human experience. I find that these parts of my life as writer, teacher, preacher, novelist, theologian, they're all very clearly one vocation for me. And my life is diminished if I'm not exploring God and the human experience in all of these different ways.

RW: I'd go along with that entirely. Occasionally people will talk to me about my poetry as though they think it is some sort of recreational activity. And it's difficult to explain that I don't just do it to unwind. Poems get written because they have to get written, because you have to get them out there. And they have to get out there because they are from somewhere very important in yourself. And if the self they're coming out of, as you say, is a self trying to say something credible, intelligent, something with integrity about God and humanity, well then, it shows. But that doesn't mean you're always writing religious poems or religious novels, let alone propagandist work. But that the continuum is undivided. The nature of the human situation you're trying to articulate and explore is one, not several. And that's hard for some people to get their minds around. I think it also explains—I don't know if you find this too—why does this or that poem not come out more positively? Or at the very simplest level: Why did you use a rude word? I had a bit of that with the Shakespeare play. I had a severe telling-off from someone who said that it was very wrong for a cleric to have people using bad language on stage.

GG: Among [some of] our Christian brothers and sisters, there is an expectation that art is going to be useful and evangelical, and I have wrestled with that, since I've published with New York publishers and progressive denominational publishers and with some evangelical publishers. An evangelical publisher put out the first edition of *Crossing Myself*, for which I remain grateful. They felt it was an important book and that the story was very much worth telling. And they also asked me to take out some bad words. The irony, of course, is that when you are writing about the worst, most painful moments in a human life, you cannot necessarily expurgate the language attached to it. I don't think I've ever told you, but when *Free Bird* first came out, the lead editor of the Christian imprint of Random House approached me about publishing what they called a Christian translation.

RW: No. Really? Good Heavens.

GG: With all the bad language taken out, and I hope nothing other than that, but the conversation that we had, which was very short, was that characters are as they are. They may be in extremis, and to ask them to behave differently, or in a less offensive manner is to rob them of the essence of who they are.

I do encounter, just as you have, people who see the creative side of you, because you are such an acknowledged theologian, as somehow pedestrian part of what you do. I have—on both sides of my writing life—people who ask me why I do the other thing. So, for example, the people who like my literary novels want to know why I waste my time writing about God. Why do you explore these things, because that is not a typical writer's career? Now Marilynne Robinson writes seriously about philosophy and theology and is a great novelist, but for the most part, you don't have that split. Then there are some folks, I think, probably fewer of these, who look at the Christian writing that I do and find it useful, and wonder why I would waste my time making up stories. So in the same way that people think your poetry is a nice sort of sideline in the hours of your day that otherwise would go unfilled.

RW: Exactly.

GG: I wrestle with that in terms of the publishing industry. I think publishers prefer to think of you as one sort of writer. I'm a literary novelist, but when editors see that I was involved in a Bible translation—*The Voice* [2011] is actually the best-selling work that comes up on Amazon when you search for me—there's a certain skepticism that literary culture has about Christian culture. And it's not unearned. A lot of Christian art is execrable, and for those very reasons that we were talking about: the flattening out of the human experience, that desire for the happy ending, which is largely around the experience of coming to faith.

Which doesn't mean that's not an important story. The novel I'm completing now is about a person who has lost faith in everything, and needs to have faith in something. But we know that that story of the person that culminates with her accepting Jesus as her personal savior—that doesn't mean that the entire life has suddenly turned around. It may be an indicator of it. But left by itself, it's bad storytelling.

RW: Bad storytelling. Going back to a phrase I used earlier, what happens in drama or fiction has to be earned. It has to have integrity on its own terms, and that's the challenge I think of representing a real conversion. Some people can do it, and I think your fiction is precisely aiming at that, just as Marilynne's *Lila* is in a sense about that. And that's a novel that a number of Christians have found difficult for the way it ends up, with a conversion to a God who's actually a good deal more risk-taking than they would like their God to be, and a God who is far too like Lila for comfort in some people's eyes. Because of that transforming recognition for Lila at the end of the novel, "I can't imagine going to Heaven without all the people who have made my life what it is. How can God imagine Heaven without them?" It's a really good way of crystallizing it, I think.

GG: Talking about my fiction and this idea of Christian translation, I don't know how much of this is conscious. Monet painted water lilies. I don't know that he necessarily got up in the morning and said, "Today I will paint water lilies"—but you have these themes that are at the heart of who you are as a writer or as a theologian, the things that resonate with you, that you come back to.

We have talked about how I was asked to cowrite a novel with Brennan Manning, *The Prodigal* [2013]. Brennan Manning preached, taught, wrote about radical love, grace, and forgiveness, and my agent

Andrea thought we should be partnered on this project because, as she said, "That's what Greg writes about. That is his language. It's his understanding of what makes life worthwhile." That can be a theological statement, but it's also a narrative statement. Brad Cannon from *Cycling*, who has decided that he's not going to live life, is actually saying that he's not going to trust in the possibility that love, grace, and forgiveness can redeem.

The fiction that I write is "Christian fiction," although it's not intended to be Christian fiction in the reductive sense of the word. Even those novels I wrote when I was outside of any faith tradition revolve around powerful sacramental moments. When we talk about pop culture later, one of the interesting things is that we have these powerful stories that work because we all share a common language and understanding. We know, for example, that confession is an essential part of our humanity. That we have to take responsibility for our failings, for the places that we have disappointed or hurt. In the Christian tradition we make it something larger still, and it has a sacred dimension with forgiveness attached to it, but it doesn't surprise me at all that I wrote a novel that ends with a formal scene of confession, which is what *Free Bird* does. There was no other way for that story to end. That character had to acknowledge what he had done—and be forgiven for it—before he could make that turning into possibility.

So for writers of faith, whether it's Marilynne or Walker Percy or P. D. James or me, whatever kind of story you have to tell is going to be demarcated by those bright touchstones of the tradition. I can't write a novel that doesn't have religious elements in it, and I don't think I would want to. That radical love, grace, and forgiveness are the things that have saved my life, and I think I'm still trying to figure out what I believe and what has been life-giving for me, and what is. Barbara Brown Taylor's question "What is saving your life today?" If you're an honest writer, whether poetry or fiction or theology, it is an ongoing exploration where you are trying to figure things out, and your hope is that in the figuring, it might be of value to the people who read.

RW: Yes. And one way or another—I think I said earlier—you don't write to solve problems, in the sense of solving problems. But you do write theology or fiction, poetry or drama, to resolve something that is actually in your heart. You do in that sense write to solve a problem. A problem of word and idea, to find a way through. And by doing that, you say to your readership, "If you find this a problem, be assured I find it one as well. If you would like to know if there's a way through, here's a thought. Here's a possible way of walking with it, or walking into it." And whether you end up in the same place, who knows? Because you're a reader and I'm a writer. You're you and I'm me. But it's that saying to the readership, "You're not wrong. This is a real issue. A real problem."

GG: And here is a way that this problem can be embodied in a human life. Which of course is one of our central theological understandings.

RW: Exactly.

GG: As opposed to saying, "This is an esoteric problem." I recognize that. Here is one of the ways it might be lived out in the form of a human life. And you can see what is successful about it and what is unsuccessful about it, and gauge your own response to it.

RW: So I think all that we've been saying is that the imaginative and the theological alike focus on that agenda. That both attempt for the writer to feel his or her way into a tangle of emotion, perception, narrative, and move through, and for the writer to say, "This matters" and there's more than one response to how it matters. The imaginative and the theological are both responses to how it matters and at what level it matters. But they're not divisible.

GG: A few years ago [2006], Marilynne Robinson won the Grawemeyer Award for Religion, the most important (and lucrative) religious prize I know, and she won it for *Gilead*. It's the sort of Nobel Prize of theology. On the one hand you could say, "But it's only a novel." On the other hand, you look at that novel, and you see how many theological expressions, how many theological themes, how many ways the characters are living out biblical narratives. That wondrous returning, retelling of the Prodigal Son story. That's one of our archetypal stories. We come back to it over and over again. And she allows us to see in these characters the working out of these themes that we wrestle with formally at the same time that she writes about a character who is a theologian, who has filled more bookshelf space than Augustine, by the way he reckons it. But most of us would not read those things on the bookshelf. That's the powerful and useful role of literature and culture, because they're universal stories we all share—and are willing to share.

Conversation Four

In Which Rowan and Greg Discuss: Writing Poetry / Writing Short Stories / Differences between Long Forms and Short Forms / *The Last Temptation of Christ* / Writing Practice / Poetic Technique / Shakespeare's Language / Faulkner / Poetry's Task: To Make You See / The Pastoral Value of Poetry

GG: Rowan, you were saying the other day that poetry is not simply a thing you do in your spare hours. And when we talked about the practice of writing for both of us, we talked about it as an essential part of who we are and what we do. I wanted to ask you about poetry. I don't write poetry. I do my very best to appreciate it, although I'm not as good a reader as I would like to be. But I wanted to talk to you about it because it is an important part of who you are, and it's something that you do really well, and I wanted to hear from you about what has led you in the direction of poetry, what comes out for you when you are writing, and I want to talk some about craft and your practice as well, because I think those could be things that are useful for all of us who wrestle with words.

RW: Well, thank you. And I'm glad you like it. I guess I started writing when I was a teenager, and like most people, writing as a teenager, I wrote copiously and badly. I've always said that if you were growing up in Swansea [South Wales] in the 1960s, then the shadow of Dylan Thomas fell very heavily across your path, and like many people, I wrote lots of second-rate Dylan Thomas imitations. I went on writing a bit as an undergraduate, and if I had to pin down a moment when it got more serious, I wrote a poem about Lazarus, I remember, as an undergraduate, and it began as poems often do, with a single image, and that was, not an image, exactly, but a moment. Imagining what would it be like to have to start to learn to breathe again. Now as Shakespeare reminds us in *King Lear*, the first time that we smell the air, we wail and cry ["When we are born we cry that we are come / To this great stage of fools" (act 4, scene 6)]. Babies have to learn to breathe. And I just suddenly thought, *Lazarus learning to breathe again*, and what you might think as the scalding sensation of breath and new life, and the poem grew around that. The conclusion, as it were, was remotely related to something C. S. Lewis says somewhere, in later life when he'd survived a near-death illness, and he said, "I sometimes think that Lazarus, rather than Stephen was the first martyr. And was Lazarus grateful to be brought back to life?" [See poem "Stephen to Lazarus" in C. S. Lewis, *Poems*, 2017.] I remember that poem, I think, because it came as some poems do, not many, as a whole, and built itself rapidly around that central question. In retrospect I don't think it was a very good poem, though it might have been the material of a good poem; I didn't have the skills, I didn't have the patience. I was writing from then on, but that was a moment when I thought, *Maybe there's something serious here, maybe I need to explore the world I'm in and the world of faith I'm in*. And that trickled on, I suppose through my twenties and thirties writing and translating a bit, the fascination of moving poetry from one language to another has really been very strong for me, as a result, partly, of growing up hearing two languages around me all the time.

But I didn't publish anything seriously until my early forties, when a small independent publisher, in conversation, asked, "I don't suppose you write poetry, do you?"

GG: Well, as a matter of fact . . .

RW: I sent him some stuff. And the rest is history. What I had done previously was to publish, along with a number of friends, little pamphlets. We exchanged poems with each other, student friends, and we'd sell them for charity. I think those pamphlets are still around somewhere. One or two of that group have gone on writing poetry and writing it seriously, but I hadn't, as I say, published anything more than that.

GG: So where did that put you in the day job?

RW: Well, I suppose through my twenties and thirties, I was a graduate student and starting to teach theology, up to when I started as a professor at Oxford. All of that was going on in the background. And I found that what I was writing was very much informed by being a teacher of theology and by being a Christian, but as I said, in a note on the first book of poetry I published, I don't want to be a Christian poet, any more, I guess, than you want to be a Christian novelist. You're a person who's seeking to exercise a literary craft, and the person you are, exercising that craft, is a Christian. So that makes a difference. Yes, of course it does. But it's certainly not at all that you try to craft something that will serve a religious purpose. It serves a religious purpose by being a good poem or a good novel, whatever it may be. That's key. I suppose since then I've gone on writing pretty regularly. People sometimes say, "Well, you must have more time to write poetry now you're not archbishop." But it doesn't work like that. The formula I use is that poetry makes the time it needs to get written. It nags at you and whines at you and pulls at your shirttails until it gets written. And it's got to come out somehow.

[W. H.] Auden, who is one of my poetic heroes, has something about finding the vanishingly elusive point between too-early and too-late with a poem. I do recognize that, that sometimes I will have a clump of words or a vaguely focused image and think, *Yeah, that's one to explore. But not just yet. It needs to simmer a bit longer.* Or changing the metaphor, the yeast needs to rise in it. Not yet. I look in my notebooks and find an idea for a poem and say, "Well, that never came to anything." And it's too late. I can't remember what that was about. So you have to find the moment or be alert to where the moment presents and then see that it gets written. As I say, just occasionally a poem will walk in, and it's really a very exhilarating experience when something presents promptly and you're almost racing to get it down before it goes away, but there it is.

There's a sonnet sequence in my first collection, and rather unusually, form and content arrived together. The first few of those I wrote very, very rapidly within a few days. And then it was a few years before I wrote the last one in the sequence. I knew that I hadn't finished it, and finally the moment came when I thought, *Yes, I think that just might tie it up.*

GG: I've had that experience with short stories.

RW: Have you?

GG: It's partly about the limited scope, at least in terms of the amount of time that it takes to write. I know our computers don't work like this any longer, but I used to think about that kind of writing in terms of Random Access Memory—you know, what was available on your old computer when it loaded up—what we're capable of handling at a given moment, in a given program, given the limitations of the computer's memory. With the short stories, there was sometimes that nagging feeling that you know the beginning, you know the ending, because there isn't that much space between. This is something that has to come sooner rather than later. There seem to be a lot of similarities between short story writing and poetry writing. The importance of language is elevated because there is so much less of it. The big difference would be that, as a short story writer, I am thinking in classic Edgar Allen Poe terms. You know: every word in this needs to be a part of the effect that I'm creating. And I would guess that, for you, it's every syllable or even every sound.

RW: There's something in that. I really appreciate the difference between writing a short story and writing a novel. I want to come back to that in a moment. But yes, you learn to listen to a poem— I'm glad you said every sound—you learn to listen to a poem and to think, *There's a dead patch there. Those sounds aren't doing anything.* You can't entirely avoid that. You notice sometimes. Or I notice it when I read something aloud, and especially when I'm reading something I wrote a while ago, I think, *Hmmm. Attention slipping there somehow. It's slacking, and the sounds aren't doing their work.* Yes, you don't have time to spare or words to spare. Which doesn't mean you're under pressure to make every word mean something in the strong sense. You've got to have a sense that the sound is there, the word is there, the sentence is there. Because of the whole.

Now if you're writing a novel, I guess, a slack patch—I don't mean a badly written patch, but a slack patch—of course the wheel has to be kept turning. I was recently rereading for the first time in ages *The Lord of the Rings* [J. R. R. Tolkien, 1954–55]. A long book. People sometimes complain about slack writing or bad writing in that, and I think, *Yes, but it's a long book, for goodness' sake. There are slack passages in War and Peace [1867].* Very interestingly, looking at Emily Wilson's wonderful new translation of *The Odyssey* [2017], she says in her introduction that an epic, of course, has dull bits, and she's not tried to make it all interesting. Homer or whoever was writing a long story, there were presumably patches where people were refilling their wine cups, stepping out to the loo, or whatever, and you knew roughly what was going on. And that just served to bulk out and intensify the moments where the narrative pitch was tightened. I thought that was very insightful, both in terms of how *The Odyssey* and *The Iliad* work, and how the writing process itself works.

GG: I think about longer forms and shorter forms by thinking of the lost art of the record album.

RW: That's a very good analogy, yes.

GG: Even in a very good album there are a couple of tracks—

RW: That are make-weights, yes.

GG: They're make-weights. You hide them in the middle of side two. But the opening track, and the opening track of side two, and the closing track of the album—they all have to be spot on, because those individual bits are the places where you make contact with your audience. I do think there is something to that. What I always tell my students is that if you're going to have slack pieces, then you're probably more of a novelist. In a short story, which is the place where I try to start my writers off, since it's a very forgiving sort of form. You can fail badly at it and get back up and try again tomorrow. But if you fail badly at a novel, then it's potentially years of your life, and hundreds of pages of effort that may or may not ever reward, except that you learn a little about how not to write a novel by writing a bad novel.

What I've discovered as someone who's worked in both forms—I haven't written short stories for a while, and that might be something I'd like to go back to, inspired by this conversation—is that when you're crafting something long, as you're saying about Tolkien, you'd love for it all to be riveting, but you also have this set of diminishing returns with the reader. We think about that in terms of emotion: I'm going to send in Macbeth to do this, and then I'm going to send in the fool because we can't handle any more of that emotion.

RW: There is a kind of elevated bad writing which tries to keep the pitch artificially high. I reread for something I was writing a few years ago [Nikos] Kazantzakis's [The] Last Temptation of Christ [1955], which I think is essentially a short story inflated to 500 pages. Kazantzakis does his best to keep the tension up all the time, but the result is that after twenty-five pages you are exhausted, and irritated. You want to say, "Cut me some slack here." It's artificially intense, and the language feels hysterical. Kazantzakis has an extraordinary imagination, he can be an extraordinary writer, and I think his other famous novel, Christ Recrucified [1948], he doesn't try to do that. The Last Temptation doesn't relax, and the result is, I think, a very bad book that is also a very significant book, a fascinating book.

GG: We said that some poems show up fully formed. What is your practice when that does not happen? How do you go in search of a poem? How do you show up for a poem, let's say, as we talked about showing up for God?

RW: Yes. If it doesn't all show up, obviously you start with what does. You get a couple of lines down. There's a wonderful idea in a poem by Charles Williams about Shakespeare, and it begins with Shakespeare on the Tube, and he imagines Shakespeare going to work in a very prosaic way ["On Meeting Shakespeare," 1925]. He's reading the newspaper, doodling in the margins, and he's just started writing *The Merchant of Venice*, and the first line of the play has come to him, and the first line of *The Merchant of Venice* is "Still quiring to the young-eyed cherubins" [act 1, scene 1]. And that's brilliant, because what Williams is saying is that the entire complex narrative structure of the play is an attempt to find a place where that line might fit.

GG: Wow.

RW: And I thought that was so good. There's an element of that in writing. You get down the phrase or the image that comes, you scribble a few things with lots of question marks. You tuck it in the back the notebook. And then from time to time you take it out and look at it. And this again is the finding the moment when it's not too early or too late, until you have, in my case, a long plane journey or train journey, or a morning you have to wait in the surgery or something like that. And you say, "Okay. Let's just see, shall we?" You tentatively open the notebook and see if it's begun to sprout, and you say, "Ah, now then. What if?" And you start just listening for a beat somewhere.

I'm fascinated by how line lengths dictate themselves. Because that's about the rhythm or beat or a poem. I've noticed that in what I've been writing the last two or three years, my lines seem to be getting shorter and a bit more attentive to syllabic regularity. I've never been a great one for strict syllabic verse counting the syllables. I try to listen for a number of beats in a line, and I've just found that I've needed in some way, for some reason, to compress my lines a bit more. So that's part of it. You try to find the beat that works, and about a year ago I was trying to finish something which, again, had come in a very messy bundle with lots of knots to untie, and I started by writing about twenty lines in a fairly straightforward blank verse. A longish line. Reading it, I thought, *That's not it. The content and the form are not meshing yet. It sounds routine. It sounds dutiful. It sounds as if I'm versifying. I've got to find a sound that actually does the work with content in another way.* I started again from scratch with a much more broken line, and a number of sections with varying rhythms and line lengths.

That, actually, is something that interests me in recent years. I've been writing rather longer pieces. Sequences. Four or five poems with a very varied voice—I don't mean in the dramatic sense—but with an opening section that would be cast in a series of three-line stanzas, a rhyming section, a rather longer and more expansive line, a section that has a faintly balladic character, and trying to pull those together. I like doing that; I like finding a way into making a poetic unity throughout those different bits of music, and if I can allude to a considerably better poet, it's what [T. S.] Eliot is doing in the [*Four*] *Quartets* [1943]. Showing you that just as with Shakespeare's plays, they talk to each other. So poetry talks to itself, prompts other ways of saying or looking or doing. To put a sequence together like that is an attempt to honor that. That is part of the craft.

The craft also involves trying to determine when, where, and how you use a very strict form and when you don't. It's easy, as has often been said, to write reams of slightly gushing prose, and then cut it up into lines that look like poetry. But to ask, "Do I want to rhyme here? Do I really want a strict syllabic sequence? Do I want a deliberately just off-key sequence?"—which is an interesting one to go for—and I can remember writing one piece initially with a fairly conventional four-line rhyming stanza and thinking, *That's got to be broken up a bit.* And working to produce what was still a tight piece in terms of its rhyme and structure, but much, much shorter, more staccato lines, that sort of thing.

GG: I brought some Baylor students over to see you from Oxford a couple of summers ago, and we sat in your music room and discussed poetry. We talked about Eliot, and we talked about some of your poems, and one of my students asked a really basic but very well-intentioned question that you answered with tremendous grace. A very beginner level sort of question, but truly, lots of people are intimidated by poetry and might wonder the same thing. She asked, "What makes a poem good?" I think many of the people reading this would like to understand poetry better, because, as we're going to discuss, there are some important links between the kind of literature we're talking about and the kind of work that people do as preachers or teachers.

RW: I can't remember precisely what I said then, but what I would say now is that a good poem is one that makes you a little more excited about language and a bit more eagerly receptive in the world. In other words, it sharpens your sensibility. It says the words we use and the things we see are more than they appear. They carry more, they embody more than we at first imagine. And to me, at the end of the day, that's a very deeply theological thing. I wrote that book *The Edge of Words* a couple of years ago [*The Edge of Words: God and the Habits of Language*, 2014], which is partly about the ways in which language, by pushing at its own frontiers all the time, itself gives us a sense of God. So I think a good poem is one that sends you away that much more exhilarated about the language that we use as a tool not just for expression, but of negotiation with the world around us.

Back to Shakespeare yet again. People love Shakespeare partly because the stories are good, the characters are profound, and partly because the language just seizes hold of you, and you think, how extraordinary that language could do this. The most compressed and unadorned—we spoke earlier about "Undo this button" or "She's warm"—to the most elaborate and also the most charged, like the language of the sonnets. I mentioned the first exchange in *Romeo and Juliet*. But I think also of the extraordinary force of some of the songs in Shakespeare's plays. I think of the balance between say, *Macbeth*, that Marlovian ambitious Latinate style of "The multitudinous seas incarnadine" [act 2, scene 2] as against "She should have died hereafter" [act 5, scene 5] and yes, you just come away from these plays thinking, *Language does that!*

GG: I remember thinking the first time I read *Hamlet*, that "To be or not to be" soliloquy, and myself a budding writer at that point,

I remember thinking, *This is life and death in one syllable words. How can you encompass so much with such simple, well-chosen language?* I find that in some of the other writers I admire, poets and fiction writers as well. Faulkner, of course, is famously ornate in his sentences, and when I teach *Absalom, Absalom!* [1936], which is a difficult book, particularly for undergraduates, they look at those sentences—of the first four sentences, three of them are over one hundred words long—but then I ask them to start going through and noticing the number of one-syllable and two-syllable words. Their eyes begin to open, and they say, okay, this is a really complicated arrangement of words. But the words themselves are really simple. I understand this word and this word and this word. That very conscious use of language is one of the things that poetry gives us.

RW: And certainly it's something that, as you say with Faulkner, some novelists do much more self-consciously than others. There's a discussion at the moment in the UK about Muriel Spark. There's a new standard edition of her novels out, and letters, and she's somebody who's famously unrelentingly spare. The novels are very, very short. And yet they're not short stories. They're novels. Or I think of William Golding, who's often thought of, rightly, as a very difficult writer. But you read each sentence, and it's not difficult. What's difficult is figuring out what's going on. It's not that the language is hard, but that the obliquity, the simplicity, of the sentence gives you a particular take on what's going on that you have to get inside to follow.

Another novelist who does that, although I don't think he's anything like as well known, although I think he's an absolute master, is Alan Garner, known mostly as a children's writer, although his adult novels have something of the Golding feel. It's not that the words are difficult. It's that the stuff is difficult. And the same lapidary simplicity, the same refusal to blather and give you any psychological insights. You've got to do the psychological spadework. It's as if a Garner or a Golding or even a Muriel Spark is saying, "I'm not going to do the interpreting of the book for you. I'm a writer. That's what I do. You're a reader." I like that in a novelist. I like being challenged, rather than being treated to too many pages of not very effective psychological analysis. There are exceptions. One of my exceptions is A. S. Byatt, who's an extremely adept reflective writer. She does it well. She knows how to do it. There are lots of people who don't, and who make the mistake of getting you inside the character the wrong way too easily.

GG: Back to this question of what makes a poem good. Language is an essential part of it, because it is the thing that makes poetry poetry. But there's, as you say, also this element that poetry helps us see. There is often this epiphanic element of something we thought we had seen, but now we see better as a result of this reading. We know better. Just as an example, you know that the overriding religious experience of my young life was growing up in a conservative evangelical tradition in which Jesus was presented as a very angry sort of savior. I now sort of understand that looking at that cross hanging over the baptistery in the Southern Baptist church where I grew up, that Jesus was essentially hanging up there 364 days out of the year. That's where he was useful. And that's why he was so angry!

I couldn't really articulate that for myself until I read a poem by the American poet Scott Cairns called "The Spiteful Jesus" [in the collections *Philokalia* (2002), *Compass of Affection* (2006), and *Slow Pilgrim* (2015)]. Scott and I are dear friends now, and I love his verse because often it explains the world to me. It shows me something I had seen before but had not understood so well. I see that in a lot of your verse as well. You talked about how you did not want to be seen as a Christian poet, and I'd guess that with a lot of poems that came out while you were archbishop, people were dumbfounded to find they weren't all religious or devotional. There's that really lovely poem "Alone at Last" [*Headwaters*, 2008], which I think is a really serious, really beautiful poem, and of course every great work of art is theological, whether or not it sets out to be devotional or religious. But there's that poem, there's the one "Unsealings: A School Play" [*The Other Mountain*, 2014], which I believe is about Pip. They're serious about the revelation in what we might think of as more pedestrian life, that is, the life that most of us operate at most of the time, as well some really profound and challenging poems, like the Shakespeare poems ["Shakespeare in Love: Ten Prospects" in *Headwaters*], which illuminate those plays in ways I had not seen before. Or the "Cambridge at 800" sequence [in *The Other Mountain*]—and I've been to Cambridge to see you many times now, but in those poems I understood the heart and soul of Cambridge in a way I hadn't walking past the colleges or jostling down Bridge Street.

RW: Well, yes. Thank you. I'm interested that you touched on "Alone at Last." I don't know where that came from. It's not 100 percent serious, but it is 100 percent serious. It's about the fallacy of thinking you're ever alone. Or you're ever just the person you think you are, and the huge array of identities—

GG: That squad of dancing characters—

RW: That's right, yes. The cliché, of course is, with someone you love, alone at last. The two people you think you are open out into a couple of dozen you are, or have been, or think each other are, and so it goes on. But it does seem to me that a good poem will show you that unexpected moment, setting, object, is, as we said earlier, more than it seems. And that's why, without I hope going into sentimental raptures about the Golden Brush of Poetry and pass over the prose of ordinary experience, forgive me, a poem will light up a room, will light up the ordinary. And if it's a poem about something extraordinarily difficult and painful, personally or collectively, then it will still illuminate. Which does not mean heal, or resolve. But it will make an experience or a memory capable of being looked at. And as I've said elsewhere, in writing about tragedy, for example [*The Tragic Imagination*, 2016], the capacity to look at and speak about the apparently unspeakable is one of those things that humans do in the face of catastrophe. I think that's why, famously, some people have said in the wake of Auschwitz, "Can you still write poems?" The response of some people, like Nelly Sachs, the great German/Swedish poet, is to say, "If we don't, then the concentration camp mentality, the death camp mentality, has won." It may be indescribably bloody difficult to write, and the risk of saying something unimaginably crass is huge, but it's a risk somehow people are being prompted to make.

GG: There is a Robert Frost poem, "Acquainted with the Night" [in *West-Running Brook*, 1928, and *The Poetry of Robert Frost*, 1970] that was really significant to me during the years I was suffering chronic depression. One of the things that any great work of art does—as we're talking about what makes a poem good—we talked about language, we talked about the explosion of meaning, but it's also, as you're saying, to look at what is most difficult about life. One of the things that the poem did for me in my most difficult times was to locate me in a human reality that said that this is something that has been experienced before. With many of the great crushing things that happen to us in our humanity, our fear is that we are alone in experiencing them.

RW: That's a key thing about language and imagination, isn't it? We waste so much time talking about creativity and self-expression, and we don't get the fundamental fact that language is our way of recognition of each other. It's the context in which we grasp that we're not alone. And that brings its own difficulties and its own catastrophes. But that's what writing is about. You're calling for recognition, and you're also offering recognition. You're saying, as you write, "Isn't this it?" And you're also saying, "This is it."

Conversation Five

In Which Rowan and Greg Discuss: The Preaching Event / Preaching Styles / Preparing to Preach / Theology of Preaching / Preaching Influences / The Sermon and the Short Story / Preaching and Healthy Self-Disclosure / The Sermon in the Context of Worship / Imagining the Lives of the Listeners / Theology and Popular Culture / Archetypal Myths in Pop Culture / Culture and Community / Embedding the Gospel in Culture / The Gospel According to *Doctor Who* / The Parables / Evangelism

GG: It strikes me that this talk about poetry and recognition offers us a place where we can make a connection with preaching, which is something we both take seriously. This past Sunday in Paris, the sermon I preached was essentially what you just said: "This is how it seems to me. Is this how it seems to you?" And of course, we're also saying, "Here's what the tradition has to offer us." But I know that both of us think of preaching as a very particular moment for a particular audience, and a big part of it is that thing we were talking about in poetry: I see where you are. We think of that in terms of the needs of a particular congregation on a particular Sunday or whatever day the preaching experience takes place. And I think another thing that translates is language: the well-chosen word, the well-chosen sound. Other things might translate for us as well.

RW: It's exactly as you describe, I think. You're trying to propose something recognizable and offer something recognizable. And as you know, one of the most moving things you can ever hear at the church door is "You might have been speaking to me." You can only think, *I hope I was. But if I was, it's not because I calculated it.* And that is one of the differences between poetry and preaching. Preaching is an event in the body of Christ. I want to give a great deal of weight to that. In some mysterious way, what is there is given in the community's life, especially but not exclusively in the sacramental gathering. I'm not expressing a set of ideas to be imposed on an audience, but in some very elusive way, connections are being made. The Spirit links up, if all's going well, with what people need to hear. You can tell when it's happening. And when it's not happening. I don't know if you've had the experience I occasionally have of preaching a sermon where you might as well have a glass shield around the pulpit, the sense the words are bouncing off and falling into a heap. How does that happen?

GG: I was talking with your wife, Jane [Williams, theologian and author]. Who you know well.

It seems that in this conversation we are often violating one of the most essential rules of dramatic writing. I always tell my students that their characters shouldn't talk to each other about things they already know. So any line of dialogue that begins "As you well know" is a bad line of dialogue. But there are some tiny bits of context that might be of value for our larger audience.

I was telling Jane last night about how often as a preacher I feel rescued by the Holy Spirit. There are those times for whatever reason when in my own attempt to gauge what a community needs, perhaps they don't need what I thought they did. There does feel to me, unlike other kinds of writing—although even there, I have a practice of prayer. As I was working on this last novel, every time I went out to my friend Terry Nathan's lake house to write I would begin sacramentally, some passages from the Psalms, and a very real prayer that the Spirit would be present and that my work might be useful—but the sacramental quality of what we do in the pulpit makes it that much more important to recognize. I long ago removed myself from any vanity that my being a good writer makes a difference necessarily to my preaching. The fact that I can move words around and find a striking image and tell a good story is an important set of tools. But if the Spirit is not present, all is in vain.

Our friend Greg Rickel [Episcopal Bishop of Olympia in Seattle, Washington] has an invocation with which he precedes every sermon, and I've taken to using it as well: "Holy Spirit, speak to us. And may we have ears to hear." Because it seems to me that that is the central thing. I can think of some sermons where I thought, *I don't know if I have found the core, and if I'm going to be of use today, if these words are going to be of use, then Spirit is going to have to step in and move underneath them like water.*

RW: Yes. That's right. That's why it isn't about style or skill of composition. It's very nice when you hear a sermon that's well-composed and well-delivered, but that's not it. You and I have both heard sermons which are formally not particularly impressive. But they get there. They get there. Which I suppose is what people like Saint Augustine are reflecting about when he talks about *sermo humilis,* the simple, the unadorned voice that preaching needs. [Augustine teaches about unadorned style in *On Christian Doctrine* 4, and about the power of simple sermons in *Instruction* 4.56; Erich Auerbach's seminal essays about *sermo humilis* are collected in his *Literary Language and Its Public in Late Latin Antiquity and in the Middle Ages,* 1965.]

I wonder how some of the really great preaching stylists of the past managed, a [John Henry] Newman or [Lancelot] Andrewes, or [John] Donne for that matter. Or Archbishop [Thomas] Tenison. [John] Tillotson. The great eighteenth-century preachers. It must have felt a bit different, and yet, looking at classical sermons, something about Donne does strike you. He's a stylist, he's a performer, he's a rock star.

GG: He's a rock star.

RW: Yet. Read that stuff aloud and it connects, because something in him is connecting.

GG: Something culturally was different. We're talking about a time that was preinternet, pretelevision, premovies. It was—not to diminish those sermons in any way—but it was also a form of entertainment. People would drop what they were doing in Oxford and go to hear Newman preach. When you're talking about Donne as a rock star, there had to be some awareness on their part that they had to keep their audience interested in some way. I think that's also true in some respects for us, although of course in our tradition, our sermons and homilies are shorter, and the question of keeping people entertained is less central. In the tradition in which I was raised, a twenty or twenty-five or thirty-minute sermon was not uncommon. If you are an African-American preacher, there's a tradition of longer sermons yet.

RW: Indeed. And in the last couple of years I preached once or twice in Afro-Caribbean or African churches, Pentecostalist churches, on behalf of our charity, Christian Aid, and I think the first time I did that in a Nigerian Pentecostal church, I asked how long, and they said, "Well, probably not more than forty-five minutes." And you're preaching in both services.

GG: Now we have heard sermons that sounded, to us, as if they were going forty-five minutes.

We were talking earlier about craft, and there is some importance to craft, because sermon writing is a form. As we've talked about poetry, drama, the novel, the short story, in every form, there are things that, historically, have worked that once you know them, then you can think about perhaps departing from them. That's why it's fair to say that a sermon can be well-crafted, although what the Spirit does with that—spirit blows where it will.

I think that may be something for pastors and priests to keep in mind. This is an event, it's liturgical, it's Spirit-led, but it's also a place where you can bring your craft to it. I have heard horror stories about people who didn't prepare to preach. Who relied on the Holy Spirit side of the equation. My homiletics professor [at Seminary of the Southwest], Roger Paynter, once told us about a preaching conference where he got up and talked about how he prepared to preach, and offered a really good, useful set of practices, some of which I use to this day. And then the next speaker got up and said, "Well, I just get up in the pulpit and say what the Spirit wants me to say." Roger told us, just to reinforce the horrified response that we were evincing, that the next person who followed that speaker, the first thing that speaker said was, "Please don't ever, EVER do that."

RW: If preaching is an event within the body of Christ, then it's an event within the Holy Trinity. In other words, it's an event in which the Word is born out of silence and activated by the Spirit. That, to me, roots it in the furthest depths in which we could possibly root it. It's all a part of that flowering out of silence which is the eternal begetting of the Word or the Son in the Divine Life. But that Word or Son always overflows through the Spirit, and in our context, overflows in this place and this time, where the word comes alive in the relation between those who are gathered as the Body. I think we sometimes sell preaching short by not plugging it into that deepest of contexts, which is the Trinitarian life. So it becomes part of how the Spirit molds a community into the likeness of Jesus Christ. And that's all about so much more than what you do with your notebook on Saturday evening.

GG: Who would you say are the people who have been most influential in your preaching life?

RW: Good question. I was very fortunate growing up to have two pastors who were both outstanding preachers, and outstanding holy people too. The first few years, as a little boy going to a Presbyterian chapel in Cardiff, my pastor's name was Geraint Nantlais Williams, from a very famous non-Conformist dynasty of scholars and preachers. He was someone who brought a very solid theological mind to bear on all this. He was somebody who had a great gift of human accessibility. Then when my family and I had become Anglicans, when I was a teenager, again Canon Eddie Hughes, our parish priest, had in the pulpit a mixture of depth and passion and warmth that absolutely reflected the person he was, the priest he was. Somebody deeply rooted in an Anglo-Catholic spirituality that wasn't in the least bit fussy or sectarian or precious, but conveyed all the time the intensity of divine love. You could warm your hands at his sermons.

I remember coming back from my first term at Cambridge, and going to Mass on a Sunday, and saying to my parents, "I've been hearing two sermons a week at Cambridge for the last eight weeks, but I haven't heard anything to touch what the vicar does."

So those two when I was a young man certainly had a big impact. And then, it's a bit different, but I listened to Archbishop Antony Bloom [also called Anthony of Sourozh], the Russian Orthodox teacher, speaking on many, many occasions, and he had the same warmth and spontaneity and theological depth, and certainly made a very big impact. Though it wasn't conventional Anglican preaching.

I do read sermons, and I do read, again and again, Austin Farrer, Farrer by common consent being one of the great Anglican preachers as well as one of the great Anglican minds of the last century. And Farrer's sermons are so beautifully crafted; they are, literally, wonders of economy and elegance of expression and theological acuity. I don't think I could preach like that now to save my life. I don't think many people could. But for Farrer, the sermon was a bit like what we were saying about the short story. He clearly thinks, *I've got twelve to fifteen minutes to say something, and it's got to be said with every single bar of the music noted.*

GG: My teacher Robert Olen Butler used to talk at the University of Iowa about the relationships between the reader and the novelist and the reader and the short story writer. It went sort of like this: If you're a novel writer, you walk up to the reader, and you take their hand, and sort of swing it, fancifully.

RW: Yes. I like that.

GG: And you tell them, "I have a story to tell you. Let's go for a walk. This may take a while. We may wander into some brambles, but we'll get out." But the short story approach is sort of like those scenes from the horror film where you grab somebody's hand and run, hand in hand, through the forest—why that happens we still do not know; it is not physically possible, I think, to run faster hand in hand—but that's the image we have of that urgency. "This is us; we are in this together; I've got a story to tell you; I don't have much time. So stick with me. Every moment matters."

RW: That's a brilliant analogy, I think.

GG: That sense of urgency. In preaching, because as you were talking about, that person comes to the back door and says, "You were preaching to me today," there have been times in my life that I absolutely needed to hear that sermon that day. And it is a hugely important thing to remember. I first walked in the doors of St. James Episcopal Church [Austin, TX] and heard a wonderful sermon by Greg Rickel, and it was precisely the sermon I needed to hear in that dark moment of my life. I am fond of saying that that church and that priest are responsible for my being on the planet today. The notion that preaching is anything other than life and death is a notion we have to resist.

RW: That's right. It certainly isn't just filling in the time. And I think that's one reason I—and you too, I believe—like Walter Brueggemann so much. Because he understands that as few people do, and writes about it with such energy and such perception.

GG: I've been very fortunate in my models. I came to preaching late, because unlike you, I really did not partake much of organized faith through much of my adult life. I came back to faith at St. James, in the early 2000s, with a set of literary tools for preaching, and that church discerned that there was something I was supposed to be doing with those gifts and sent me off to seminary. There I had the chance to formally learn some things about preaching from Roger Paynter, from Charlie Cook, who was my pastoral theology professor, and Cynthia Briggs Kittredge, the great New Testament scholar, but I think a great deal of what I learned about preaching, I learned from Greg in St. James parish. And the biggest thing I learned from him was about preaching in your authentic voice. Greg never pretended to be anything other than what he was. He brought his own experience to every bit of exegesis, every sermon that he preached, but there was an authenticity about everything that he did that I still try to emulate.

There are other preachers I admire. Barbara Brown Taylor is one of the great preachers of our time, and I remember a sermon that she preached at the seminary using one of the Daily Office texts, a text so bad we don't use it in the lectionary. This horrible text—I don't remember what it was now, I wish I did; she could probably tell you—she came in and preached one of the five greatest sermons of my life from this horrible text we don't even use on Sunday. It was absolutely perfect for our community at that moment. She has these amazing literary gifts and is one of those rare people who has both those gifts and the ability to preach into a moment.

The other person that I really admire—although I never knew him, he did go to Seminary of the Southwest for his Anglican training—was John Claypool, one of the great preachers in the Baptist tradition, and then one of the great preachers in the Episcopal Church. I often read those sermons he preached on the illness and death of his daughter [*Tracks of a Fellow Struggler: Living and Growing through Grief*, 1995]. The thing I carry away from them which I have taken and made a part of my preaching aesthetic is his radical honesty.

At a clergy retreat I did in the Diocese of Olympia a couple of years ago, a priest articulated how we might best use our personal experience. She said something like, "We preach out of our scars, not out of our wounds."

RW: Ah. Yes.

GG: With the idea being that we have some sort of understanding of what's going on, as opposed to, I am bleeding at this moment.

RW: That is a key distinction. isn't it? A key distinction. And I think it goes back to what we were saying about poetry and the novel too, about the challenge to say and see something. The tragic dramatist doesn't say, "God, this is awful," and nothing else. A structure of moving with it and holding it somehow. And I think it is a distinction not every preacher gets clear. I remember one of my old students working in a parish as a priest. The parish priest was someone going through a hideously difficult time, and the trouble was that the presentation of himself as a priest and preacher sucked everything around him into the vortex of his own unhappiness and frustration and tragedy. His struggles with faith, his struggles with a dysfunctional family, personal tragedy. And everything in the community became about that somehow. Now that's how not to do that. That's the wound.

GG: And that becomes the sort of preaching as therapy. And not a kind of good therapy for anybody.

RW: No, that's something one doesn't do. It's true one preaches to oneself, that's an important thing. In other words, you identify in yourself those things that need to hear those aspects of the gospel. But that's very different from preaching yourself. You're looking for where the gospel has traction, not just what your problem is.

GG: And not just my easy resonating take with the gospel, because I have a sermon I could preach week after week, regardless of the Gospel text.

RW: Oh yes. I think that's why it also helps us to have a lectionary. To have more than one reading on a Sunday. To be reminded all the time that you can't just recycle the same thing. You've got to make some token effort to relate to it.

GG: Yes. Make a stab at it, if you would.

RW: In the old prayer book, of course, the Epistles and the Gospel were not always thematically related in any way you can discern, so it's quite a virtuoso task sometimes to bring them together. And I always admire preachers who could bring them together. Austin Farrer could do that.

GG: I think we are trusting that in the readings, in the liturgy, and in the sermon there is an interaction and Spirit is moving—

RW: The sermon does not have to do it all. The commentary on the biblical text is the entire liturgy. And the community's life, too.

GG: Sometimes there's something in the collect or elsewhere that resonates beautifully with what you said. And sometimes it picks up something you didn't say.

RW: Yes. I've often had the experience of sitting down from preaching and someone gets up to do the intercessions, and my first thought is, *Oh yes. I didn't think of that, did I?* And that may be something in the intercessions responding to the lections or the general context of this community in this time, or society at this time. When I'm on top of it, at least I don't feel as though, "God, I failed. That was an awful sermon." I think, *I said something, now somebody is saying something else. That is perfectly right and proper. That's what this event is about.*

GG: Let me ask one thing before we depart from preaching. Parish priests are among the busiest people I know. And you are one of the busiest people I know.

We talked about your practice with poetry. We talked about my practice with novels, which is to go away and exit my life for a whole. But how, in the midst of busyness, are you able to write a sermon? Is there a practice you employ?

RW: Well, I have to confess that I very seldom write a sermon. I am reliably told that I am much more intelligible when I talk than when I write, which I do believe. My heart always sinks a bit when somebody says, "We'd like the text in advance," or in the days when I had my former job and there would be national set-pieces and the BBC would be recording the service, you had a certain amount of time allotted it, and you knew it would be trolled through by the media.

Edit, edit, edit. Reread. Look for bear-traps. I'm very glad I don't have to do that now.

But the practice is, ideally, to make sure that the readings are in my mind well in advance, at least a week. A preliminary reading, which will, I hope give me some hook on which to hang reflection, and then at odd moments in the days leading up, just let that swing around a bit inside, see what it gathers. But usually it's not until the day before I try to put a structure together in my mind. And even then, I find that sometimes when I've got to the church and I've started preparing myself more directly for the service, something else will very slightly change the shape of it. I've always liked to arrive reasonably early in church if I'm preaching and spend some time in quiet in that place with the people arriving. I find a corner and just sit. Because I need to arrive there. And it sounds a bit wooly, but I need to absorb the place. I need to breathe the same air as the people. And even if it's as simple a thing as saying a few words with the people as they come in, before I sit down, it's that attempt prayerfully to open up to what's going on between God and God's people in that moment in that place. And that's often the moment when I pray quietly at which something will click, and a shape which was reasonably clear in my mind will suddenly come into sharp focus and I think, *That's how to start. That's the point. That's the way in.*

I'm told by one or two kind commentators that my biggest problem preaching is how to finish a sermon. And I do know sometimes, I hear myself having said what I've got to say and not knowing how to let go of it, and blathering on a bit—

GG: How to stick the landing, we might say.

RW: That is hard. If you're preaching, as I tend to, without a written text in front of you, I find that's the hardest thing. Finishing. Have I said it? Is that clear? What do I want to leave them with? On a good day, so to speak, I'll have thought of that. I know in my mind where I want to end up. On a bad day, when I haven't prepared as fully as I should do, that's the biggest problem.

GG: I will tell you that sitting there in the church and soaking up may sound wooly, but that was also the advice my homiletics professor gave us. And particularly when you're coming into a community—

RW: That you don't know all that well.

GG: He talked about how he worked even in his own church, where he knew the parishioners well. He would go out and sit in the various pews and imagine the lives of those people, what they needed to hear, what good news they needed at that moment, and I have found that really valuable as a practice. I've carried it over into my teaching as well, because I've not sure if you've noticed it here at Cambridge, but in the States our students seem to be considerably more fragile emotionally—

RW: Oh yes.

GG: In my Harry Potter class this spring, out of fifteen people, a good half were wrestling with mental health or emotional issues. To think about where they are and what they're wrestling with besides reading for class shaped the way that I taught, and it shapes the way that I preach.

RW: I think that's crucial, because coming back yet again to preaching as an event in the body of Christ, it does mean that you're not going to be preaching with any Spirit presence unless there's that basic empathy with where people are. And with all the appropriate differences clocked, the same applies to teaching. The moments I think when I've been most called to account as a teacher, over many years, are the moments when somebody says, "You weren't thinking when you said that. How that would sound to me, or to somebody else." And that might be a woman or a person with a disability or something like that. People will sometimes say, "I know you didn't mean" whatever, but . . .

GG: But.

RW: Listen to yourself. Strange, isn't it, that to learn empathy you don't just listen to the other, you listen to yourself. Or you listen to yourself through the ears of another. And in that process discover where you're putting up the barriers, you're putting up the obstacles to learning or listening.

But you mention Harry Potter, and I wonder if that's a moment to move on to the popular culture set of things we wanted to talk about. You have—I was going to say that you've carved out a niche for perceptive and thoughtful theological commentary on different aspects of popular fiction and popular culture. That's something that clearly has come through both an evangelistic impulse and out of your own regular teaching.

GG: There's a story I often tell when I'm speaking in a diocesan or parish setting about religion and culture, and it's a story that comes from the dark days of my chronic depression. Probably the worst time in my life was the year 2000. I came very close to dying that summer as I was writing *Free Bird* in Santa Fe, New Mexico, and several times that fall after my wife left me and if felt like every part of my life had fallen apart. Of course, 9/11 happened then on top of everything else, and I was thinking, *God, if you are there, are you kidding me? Because I'm not sure that I can take anything else.* But I prided myself on the fact that I was still functional enough to get out of bed and drive from Austin to Waco and teach my students, because I loved my students, and I took that responsibility so seriously, and it is not too much to say that it kept me alive in that difficult time.

But there was a Tuesday morning after 9/11 when I was on the interstate driving north from Austin, and I could not do it. It became clear to me that I had reached the end of my strength, my capabilities. It was like that moment in a movie where one of the characters in a movie tells the others, "Go on without me. I'm done for. Save yourselves."

I pulled over to the side of the road, cars whooshing past at seventy, seventy-five miles an hour, and I was weeping so hard that I could not see. It was like being in a driving rainstorm.

And then at that moment, a song by U2 came on the radio, the great Austin station KGSR, bless them, and it was the song "Beautiful Day." We talked about how the sermon can be life or death. I believe, as I know you do, that Spirit moves in multiple ways. That there are all sorts of sacraments in this life. Many times in my life, as in this story, I have been spoken to through the culture, through stories, through films, and, on this day, through music. And I was listening to the song, which I knew well. The album [*All That You Can't Leave Behind*, 2000] had come out that fall, it was all over the airwaves because it was America's post–9/11 coping mechanism, these beautiful songs. "Beautiful Day" and "Stuck in a Moment You Can't Get Out Of." Even for very secular people, those songs were bits of grace as they were trying to make sense of themselves and the broken world.

In the bridge of that song, Bono is singing about looking at the world from outer space: "See the world in green and blue / See China right in front of you"—and then in the last part of the bridge, it's "See the bird with a leaf in her mouth / After the flood, all the colors came out." When I heard those two lines, and reckoned back to the Flood, that moment in our biblical story when everything fell apart, when disaster struck, and yet—there was some grace on the other side of it. "After the flood, all the colors came out." I heard that, and I stopped crying, and I put the car in drive, and I went another day. And another day. And another day.

When I tell that story—which I can still hardly tell without breaking into tears, because it's such a potent memory for me—I always ask people in the congregation or in the audience, "Do you have a story like that?" And of course, everyone does. A song that they heard in a moment when it made sense of the world for them, or a movie that struck them at a particular moment. So what I think—and I've got theological vocabulary for this now since seminary—it's this idea that revelation continues, and that grace continues to be distributed, not just through the formal sacraments, and not just through the sermon, and not just through the holy actions of God's people. But through the holy productions of human beings.

RW: Yes.

GG: Augustine says, "Whatever is true and beautiful is of the Lord" [*On Christian Doctrine* 2]. The way I think of this theologically— and the early fathers had a lot more language connected to this—but if you encounter something that is True and Beautiful, it somehow brings you back toward the author of Truth and Beauty.

RW: Yes. Yes.

GG: You can make a case for a rock and roll band from Ireland being an instrument of God's grace. You can make a case for Quentin Tarantino.

RW: Yes.

GG: You do not have to be formally claimed by any religious tradition—I don't know that anyone is claiming Tarantino—but we've talked about how that distinction between the sacred and the secular is, in some ways, specious. Spirit can move in all sorts of ways.

The reason I'm so drawn to this work. First, for me, it has been literally life-saving. In my own journey, during those long arid periods when I was outside of any church tradition, it was *Pulp Fiction* [1994], or the music of U2, or the novels of Walker Percy that kept me in some sort of continued being, and I know that is true for others as well. And as you mentioned, it's an evangelical way that I think about this work, not in the sort of "I'm going to use you to preach Jesus," but in the sort of way that it is possible, because we are all spiritual beings, to make these universal connections. We are all looking for Home. We are all looking for Community. We are all looking for something larger than ourselves that we can give ourselves to. And those are the stories of our faith, but they're also the great stories we tell over and over again.

RW: It oughtn't to surprise, but if we are serious about the doctrine of Creation, creation isn't something God did a long time ago. It's something God does now as we're speaking. You might say that occasionally in the pulpit: "God is creating the world now." And now. And now.

Therefore, God is not absent from the world, because it is the divine energy that is throbbing in every moment. When human beings are to some degree opened up by pain, by love, by compassion, by dread, by any number of things, what they're opening to is that More than You Thought, which is at the heart of the world, and that More than You Thought opens ultimately onto the energy of God. So, yes. Not just that creativity in the rather glib sense of finding interesting things to do with your imagination, but that desperate creativity which comes from the brokenness of great joy and great grief. Well, to use the biblical language, the fountains of the deep are opened [Genesis 7:11] and something wells up, something comes through, like it or not.

Many theologians have compared the action of God's grace to water. It finds its way in. It finds its way somewhere. If there's anything it can get through, any cranny or gap, it will be there. It's that underlying pressure, the fountains of the great deep, which underlies our human experience, and is always pushing to be through, and—well, it is remarkable, isn't it, how we go back to these images of water and flood and rain and immersion to speak of both grief and grace. "The waters have come up to my neck," says the psalmist [Psalm 69:1, NRSV], or "The waters are coming even unto my soul," in the old translation, the old wonderful mistranslation. We talk about baptism, for goodness' sake. And I think of that—do you know that hymn "Lord Jesus, Think on Me" [Translator: Allen William Chatfield; Tune: Southwell]? It's an ancient hymn by Synesius of Cyrene, the well-known Patristic writer. The last verse of it always brings me up short:

> Lord Jesus, think on me
> That, when the flood is past,
> I may the eternal brightness see
> And share Thy joy at last.

And somehow—I don't know what it is about that image, when the flood is past—you have that sense of, you know, the waters stilling and subsiding, and something appearing slowly, quietly, into the light and the brightness. I really don't know why that verse always clutches at me.

GG: We are telling and retelling these universal stories, and what I love about it is that often, sadly, if you will, great writers, great artists, are telling our stories more compellingly than we are telling them. One of the early pieces of my coming back to faith was the first book that I wrote about popular culture, the book that I wrote with my friend Chris Seay on *The Matrix*. I know you've been thinking a lot about Christology of late, and I was assigned the chapter on Neo [Keanu Reeves] as Christ-figure. For the first time in many, many years, I had to ask myself not just the question "How is Neo a classic Christ figure?"—which is a literary question you can ask yourself—but I had to start asking myself, "Who is Jesus?" Which for me was the jump from, okay here is an archetypal story about human sacrifice and compassion and all of those things that are tied up in the archetype of Christ which make the Jesus figure such a compelling literary trope. But that recognition of it in the film made me start asking the spiritual question—

RW: Who is it who is at the heart of that paradigm? What's the story that makes all these other stories have that shape?

GG: It was a very important part of my coming back to faith. More of the intellectual stuff. What happened to me at St. James was liturgical and communal. I was rescued by them, I found a mentor in the faith, and I found a community that practiced radical hospitality, which was what my bruised soul needed. And a community that was outer-focused, which was, *Once we have patched you up, you have a job to do. We all do.* But the early parts of it, were I to give my testimony, as we used to call it in the Baptist church, this is what it would sound like. Thus a huge part of it is attached to the stories that I've consumed that have made me think. Which is one of the reasons that I think this work is really important. When I'm writing about zombies, or about Harry Potter, or the ways that we've understood the afterlife, or any of these other projects, I always like to think of laying breadcrumbs back to the tradition.

RW: Yes. I like the breadcrumbs.

GG: Not in the sense that I'm saying, "Here is Neo, and here is Jesus. Don't you love Jesus?" Asking them to reflect on the myth we see expressed and the truth the myth expresses and asking, "What can this be for you in terms of your own journey?"

RW: It connects, doesn't it, with the famous conversation that C. S. Lewis had with [J. R. R.] Tolkien which really precipitated his conversion, the idea that there is one myth which is also fact, and it's because of that fact that so many myths are generated. They take you back there. At some moment, that fundamental story of absolute redemptive self-emptying restoration happened in some utterly prosaic material location in the ordinariness of a humanity, that ever-lasting fact took place. And because of that, yes, the light shines back from here and here and here in all sorts of forms. You look at the central story through the prism of a song, a drama, a story, a film, and you come away with both the perceptions enriched.

GG: What also happens, particularly happens for people of faith, is that the popular culture can speak back to our tradition. You can read Matthew's Discourse on Life in the Faithful Community [Matthew 18] and you can see what the writer of Matthew has to say about how we're supposed to live with each other. Or you can read an amazing story about a community in action.

One of the things that I carried away from the U2 book was how for forty years, during most of which time they have been outside of organized religion (I think Bono is popping back in now for some sacraments), but they have been a sacred community for each other. What our pop culture and literary stories allow us to do is see our stories acted out and embodied. We look at this band. You and I both have been married—you much longer than I, and until very recently, much more successfully—we know that it's hard to live in a marriage. But I've also been in rock bands, and in a rock band you are married to each of the other members. To see that faithful community, how people get along and work together for something larger than themselves, an ecclesia, I learned an incredible amount about what I should be doing in Christian community through the story of U2.

RW: Revelation coming up: I've never been in a rock band. That will surprise our readership. The nearest I've come, I suppose, is as a school student and college student doing a fair amount of both acting and singing, and the sense that a really good experience in theatre can give, that you are absolutely interdependent with the people you are onstage with, there is no way in which you can shine at their expense if you want this to be what it must be. The remarkable kind of—what's Donne's image, the eyebeam crossing ["The Ecstasy"]—when you meet someone's eye onstage when you're singing or you're acting and you know this is working. Once I was singing in a concert, I must have been twenty-three or twenty-four, doing a duet with a particularly good soprano soloist, and we were doing a duet in a Mozart Mass. Soprano/bass duet. Just one moment when our eyes met across the stage, a moment of absolute mutual joy. Yes, this is working. A little bit of what you're talking about resonates there for me.

GG: In stories, we learn from characters by watching them make ethical decisions, watching them fail or succeed.

RW: That's right.

GG: It's a way of taking chances without taking them personally. I don't have to fail in this spectacular fashion. Now. I can find another way to fail.

RW: But, to see, to follow the story of someone failing and recovering, to *recognize*, to use that important word again, to realize what is happening, that's how our imagination and our faith are planted together in these contexts.

We did say we'd talk about *Doctor Who* at some point.

GG: Let me throw one thing in here first because I'll forget it. It strikes me that there's an interesting dimension in our interaction with people who are artists of faith. If something is True and Beautiful, then it's specious to distinguish whether it was intended to be written for sacred or secular purposes. But we also have favorite writers, musicians, filmmakers who are consciously on a spiritual exploration. In your poems, in my novels, in the films of Terrence Malick, the novels of P. D. James—

RW: Walker Percy, who you mentioned, is important to me too.

GG: I like to talk about J. K. Rowling's faith, because in America, and I guess around the world, the Potter books are banned by fundamentalist groups in every tradition. But I am fond of talking about how I met her bishop at the Edinburgh Festival of Books, and how early on, during interviews for the first book [*Harry Potter and the Philosopher's Stone* / *Harry Potter and the Sorceror's Stone*], she told reporters that she was a person of faith, that her children were christened in the Church of Scotland, how she goes to church for more than weddings and funerals, and how the entire shape of the Harry Potter epic was shaped by the Christian gospel narrative. Even my students at Baylor are startled by this sometimes. When we begin to pay attention to the intentionality of it—she saves the overt Christianity for book seven [*Harry Potter and the Deathly Hallows*], and the two Bible verses which appear in the graveyard where Harry's parents are buried—she told MTV (because you tell MTV these sorts of things) that those Bible verses were the thematic core of everything she did in Harry Potter. [Matthew 6:21 (NRSV): "For where your treasure is, there your heart will be also"; 1 Corinthians 15:26 (NRSV): "The last enemy to be destroyed is death."]

When we look at the conscious use of Christianity by artists that we love—it's one of the things I love about U2, one of the things I love about Percy, because he made it possible for me to know what it was like to wrestle with doubt and live in a very complicated world—there's a special gift that we get from literature and culture that shares some of our assumptions about how the cosmos operates and what we're doing here.

RW: Indeed.

GG: Some years ago, in one of our early visits at Lambeth Palace, you said to me, "If I wrote the sort of books that you write, I think I should write something about *Doctor Who*." I would point out, that out of the 2011 Holy Week Lectures at Canterbury, you have written this really good book about C. S. Lewis [*The Lion's World*, 2012], exploring the literary and theological dimensions of *The Chronicles of Narnia*. You and I are both huge fans of the show, although I haven't watched it of late, and at that time the show was in its renaissance.

RW: Absolutely. Its golden age.

GG: There is something to be said about our paying attention to works that are popular, because when something is hitting something in the zeitgeist it's important to understand it as human beings. Then for those of us with a religious vocation, it's important to understand why they're so popular. It's why I wrote that book about the Zombie Apocalypse [*Living with the Living Dead*, 2017].

Why is this currently the most popular narrative in the world? I want to understand this.

So what was it about *Doctor Who* that made you think, there's a theological dimension to this that deserves to be explored?

RW: I think in the great seasons of the early renaissance, particularly in some of David Tennant's early work [Tennant played the Tenth Doctor from 2005 to 2010], and when Russell T. Davies was heavily involved, there was a sense that this show was a vehicle to explore profound moral questions. A vehicle for exploring the cost of moral decision-making. It was very courageous. It pushed boundaries. It famously, in one episode, even allowed you to see a Dalek from the inside. [The Daleks are *Doctor Who*'s most famous villains, a race of cyborg aliens whose primary drive is to exterminate all other life.] It would raise questions about doing evil that good may come, raise questions about whether one human life was a price you were prepared to pay for the salvation of the world, a kind of Ivan Karamazov question, and the Doctor in these contexts didn't appear as a uniformly right or good figure. And that was interesting because the Doctor was making those decisions sometimes and bearing the cost.

I remember one of the David Tennant episodes where the prime minister, Harriet Jones, played by Penelope Wilton, isn't it, orders the destruction of an alien fleet as they retreat from Earth ["The Christmas Invasion," 2005], having given assurances because she wants to do what she's there to do, which is absolutely to secure her people, and the Doctor turns on her. That sort of moment really does enlarge the moral space that we are in. I think that's what I loved about those. They were funny, they were hugely inventive, and they were brave in that respect.

GG: One of the sayings of C. S. Lewis that I love from his literary criticism is how fantastic literature—and I would certainly include science fiction there as well—allows us to, as he says, steal past the watchful dragons of reason. [C. S. Lewis, "Sometimes Fairy Stories May Say Best What's to Be Said," *New York Times,* November 18, 1956, and in *Of Otherworld: Essays and Stories*, ed. Walter Hooper (New York: Harcourt Brace & Jovanovich, 1966), 37.]

RW: That's right.

GG: So many of those stories were ethical stories about what it was like to live in a post–9/11, post–7/7 [the terror bombings of the London Underground took place on July 7, 2005] world. You mentioned the one with the prime minister. I think of the episode where a future Britain is in outer space on the back of a suffering space whale, which sounds ridiculous on its surface—

RW: But.

GG: But. The basic premise of the story is that the continued survival of Britain is contingent on the continued torture of this sentient being. It is a way of asking those really hard 9/11 questions that we often did not ask ourselves outside of those stories. There was never in the United States, for example, as there was in this country, any debate about torture and rendition. For the most part, even in the last election—and we're going to talk about faith and politics shortly—there was surprisingly little discussion when our now-President [Donald] Trump announced that he would bring back waterboarding and worse. In fact, polls in the US after 9/11 showed that evangelical Christians, particularly Christians who attended worship rather more often, were more in favor of the idea of torture if it kept America safe. How we square that with our worship of a savior who was tortured and put to death by an imperial state, I do not know. But to be able to enquire of those practices in these stories—as J. K. Rowling also does in the later Harry Potter novels—

RW: She does indeed.

GG: Torture becomes a very important story element in book five [*Harry Potter and the Order of the Phoenix*], and there's much more commentary, embedded within this fantasy narrative so you don't have to make the transference to, Yes, I'm talking about policies supported by Tony Blair and George W. Bush. But you can make that transferal, and you can look at the story and say, "This is horrible. I do not approve of this. I do not like it when Harry Potter is tortured, and perhaps I would not like it when other people are tortured."

So I love that you've identified that moral questing. Of course, that's what we find in all great stories. You've shared this book *Tyrant* by Stephen Greenblatt with me, and it talks about how Shakespeare's plays deal obliquely with the political issues of his day, but deep down he is dealing with them. And Greenblatt in his book, as he talks about how Shakespeare deals with political issues in his day, is obliquely dealing with the issues of ours. It allows you to take it on if you are ready to take it on, or to skate over it if you are not.

The important work that people of faith, and particularly people who have a responsibility in the pulpit or as teachers or as writers might have in connection with the culture is to interrogate it. So we can identify those themes in a way that is of use to the people we serve. That's why I think that continues to be such important work for me. I believe in it not just because the culture was—and still is— an important part of my own faith journey. But because there's that practical value that it allows us to talk with people who may not share much with us except those stories.

RW: Yes. That's fascinating, isn't it? In a culture where we have far fewer common narratives than would have been the case three or four hundred years ago, what narratives there are, what vernacular songs there are, what gives us a common culture of sorts, I think the Christian ignores them at their peril. Because that's the ground where you have to start, that's where you have to be present. It's no good imagining that you can just parachute into that world, or indeed, that the gospel itself can be parachuted in.

That's a mistake we often make, isn't it? Because we rightly believe that the gospel is, it's not just a version of something else, not a metaphor for something else, it is what it is absolutely, we can make the mistake of thinking we don't have to make any connections. We don't need to do what the writers of the New Testament are doing all the time, which is to bed it in, whether into the Jewish world or the Gentile world. To do the job of saying, "This took place in order to fulfil what was written in the scriptures." Or to do what Paul is doing in Acts 17 with the men of Athens [Acts 17:16–34]. They don't think you could just parachute in.

GG: It's also what Jesus is doing in the parabolic teachings.

RW: Preeminently, yes.

GG: Jesus is saying to them, "I can't explain to you what the kingdom of God / heaven is like"—

RW: "But you know this?"

GG: "Here's a thing." So try this on. Or try this on. Or try this on. And maybe one of these stories, which is embedded here in the first-century Palestinian world, will hit for you.

RW: So striking that the parables are secular stories. They're not stories that mention God. They're stories in which God is mentioning the world.

GG: So here are these foolish bridesmaids. Or here's the farmer who puts the plow to the ground and turns to look backward. They're all things that speak in the language and story of that particular culture. And that's what we're called to do in this culture.

RW: The parable link is a really helpful category, I think. Not otherwise a very good book—so I'd better not mention it—but one which made the point that Jesus's own use of parable made the Church see his life as parable. That is, Jesus's own use of the narratives of persons of this world to speak God help people to see that Jesus as an event in this world, spoke God. And encourage them, therefore, not just to tell people about Jesus and his teaching, but to tell a story. And to tell the stories he did.

GG: A last practical thing for people in the Church. I hear you, I think echoing this call to engage with the culture. There are Christian subcultures who find the world very frightening, and a Christian ghetto gets built behind the walls, and sadly what thrives there is often Christian music, literature, and art for people who already carry all the same suppositions. But you mentioned early on that there is an evangelical element to engaging the culture, and I am sometimes called by critics "evangelical," although I'm not evangelical in the sense that I was raised, where I was taught to walk up to people on the streets, say hello, and ask, "Have you met Jesus?"

But I am evangelical in the sense that I understand the grace of God as mediated by Jesus to be the thing that has saved me and is saving me, that is the central part of my identity and how I understand myself. There are really profound ways that I can tell that story through the cultural echoes of it, and there are ways in which people will respond, often very positively to that, where they wouldn't respond to the stranger walking up on the street who tries to tell me how to live my life.

One of the cultural things that has been powerful in the Episcopal Church is the U2charist, which we've talked about in the past. I've preached at some, played at some, which was a great joy if a reminder that I'm no longer anywhere near the guitarist I once was. But a lot of people talked about how Jesus People and Bono People have shared DNA. You can put them in the same room and they're going to discover a shared passion for justice and community. They're going to be able to speak to each other.

The simple fact of your church hosting a U2charist or hosting a film series on race and prejudice—there is something profound and powerful about opening sacred space and offering there a common experience of our culture and then mediating it in some way. As somebody who has seen the practical efficacy of this, to do it not because it'll necessarily increase your pledging units, but because this is a way to bring people inside the walls who might otherwise remain outside. What they're going to do with this connection, this encounter, is up to the Spirit. But if we do believe God is revealing God's self in these ways as well as in the formal sacraments, this is a manifestation of the work of evangelism that cannot be ignored.

Conversation Six

In Which Rowan and Greg Discuss: Faithfulness in Political Life / Bonhoeffer's Ethics / Immigration in the States / A Faithful View of Humanity / Political Tribalism vs. Faithful Engagement / Abortion / Rights vs. Responsibilities / Failure as Humane / Guns / MLK / The Hope of the Christian

GG: Well, I think the last of the big areas that we had said we wanted to talk about was this conjunction of faith and politics. How do people of faith understand their relationship with power? What sorts of things are people of faith called to be doing at any given time? While I don't think I've ever stood any nearer to power than being the student council president in high school, you have been within arm's-length of a few people over the years, and people actually assumed that being archbishop granted you a certain amount of power, although it was really power to chase eighty million cats.

RW: Exactly, yes.

GG: But you have written a book called *Faith in the Public Square* [Bloomsbury, 2012], and think an awful lot about these questions of how we are both faithful and called to some sort of action.

RW: Yes, and I think any Christian thinking about this is going to be stuck from the word "go" because it's very clear that the fundamental model of the New Testament is that God's way of changing things is failure, and unplanned failure. It's as if the New Testament just plops that down in front of us and says, "Well, that's how it works," so you can't really deduce anything very systematic from that. That's why I think Christians get in a bit of a muddle when they reflect on politics, because if you say, "Well, okay then, the thing to do is nonviolence and all the rest of it." If that's your way of succeeding, then don't expect it to be any better. Likewise, you have people who say, in effect, "Well, the Sermon on the Mount is all very well, but Jesus couldn't have meant what he said, so let's just do the realpolitik." That's not good enough either. This is where somebody like David Bentley Hart is so appropriately shocking and challenging. He writes in his introduction to his translation of the New Testament that there is just not going to be a system that will make this work. Therefore, there is not going to be, I think, for Christians, a big broad-brush political ethic. There is just going to be a human ethic. And sometimes it works and sometimes it doesn't. And sometimes you make compromises, and sometimes they fail, and that's where, for me, the most illuminating presence in the twentieth century is [Dietrich] Bonhoeffer.

Not just his heroic witness, but also the way he writes in his book on ethics, the fragments on ethics I should say, which he was writing in the end of his life [*Ethics*, 1949]. The way he writes there about the penultimate goods, the ultimate things; the fundamental structures are there, and we're always making quite complicated and iffy decisions about what will serve those ultimates. And what we mustn't expect is justification. That is to say, we can engage, as he *well* knew, in more or less virtuous political action, but what we can't do is produce a scheme which tells us, this is how you can be right, wherever you are.

That's why, although I have always been, and still am, on the political left, I'm very cautious about elevating Christian socialism or something like to the status of a universally valid principle, because we're just going to go on getting it wrong. There's something about power itself which scripture simply queries. It doesn't push it down and tramp all over it, it just says, "Really?" with any settlement we reach. So the effort—Bonhoeffer again—is to try and keep your eyes with integrity on the ultimates, to be uncompromisingly honest about the failures en route, the delusions, and, as he says, to hand it over to

Christ. Which is not at all a recipe for pacifism or political inactivity, it's just a caution, as he says, against a kind of political messianism.

GG: One of the tendencies that we have as a Christian family is to look at the same situation and see it differently based on our reading of scripture. Sometimes it's not even people who are far removed from each other exegetically. I think of the Niebuhrs [brothers Reinhold and H. Richard and their sister Hulda]—

RW: Yes.

GG: —Thanksgiving dinner at the Niebuhr family where they're arguing about pacifism and the role of society to create some sort of Christian good. So I wonder, what is a way for us to read scripture responsibly, do you think, that allows us perhaps to come to some agreement about what the Bible *really* has to say to us, and what it *really* is that we're supposed to be doing?

RW: At the heart of that, I guess, is what scripture has to say to us simply about being human, being in the image of God, before God, called by God, answerable to God. That's the human being God made, God is concerned with, God wants to see live and flourish. So when you take, corporally or individually, ethical decisions, collective decisions, personal decisions, you're thinking, partly, how does this act enhance or otherwise that fundamental place of human beings: before God, called by God, answerable to God. And if you find yourself in a situation where you can't see a clear way there, then make sure you say so. Make sure you recognize it.

GG: Yes.

RW: Don't pretend. In the classical political standoffs between freedom and security, the question is not, "Is there an all-time right answer?" For example: absolute freedom of speech is the supreme good in every situation. A classic liberal position. I think Christians, like a good many other ethicists, would say absolute freedom of speech is a good. It's an unmistakable good.

GG: Right.

RW: If that good is pursued and exercised in a way which is finally disempowering and demeaning, then you pay that price. Is that all right? To treat freedom of speech as an absolute good can *only* happen if we pay the price of certain people's suffering. Are we prepared to pay that price? If not, we have to pay the price of absolute freedom of speech, so it's keeping in view, I think, what best serves the long-term interest and well-being of the human beings who are there.

So, in the freedom of speech instance, I would say it's perfectly proper for governments to limit and to punish hate speech, to say that the absolute freedom to say of the racial, religious, or sexual other that they're something less than human is a freedom that has to give way to the need for those marginal voices not to be silenced. In other words, that would serve the longer-term goal of a public conversation in which every voice is audible, rather than a public conversation where somebody is about to shut someone else down. Roundabout way of putting it, but you see what I mean.

Likewise, I think in the ethics war, my instincts are largely pacifist and I am definitely a nuclear pacifist, in the sense that I cannot conceive a just nuclear war. It's literally unthinkable. There could be no justification for the indiscriminate human and environmental wreckage that would mean. But I find, again along with Bonhoeffer, I can't simply say, every imaginable conflict is wrong. And the just war tradition has not completely lost its substance. There are cases where it seems we have to take the risk, the large moral risk, of intervening for someone's protection, say, or our own. As the world gets more complicated in its military technology, the number of situations in which that risk is worth taking diminishes all the time, because conflict is so easily accelerated and so lethally accelerated these days.

GG: One of the things that I think could be helpful to us is just the reminder that it's important to read the Bible well when we're seeking a contemporary answer. At the time of our conversation, we're a week or two out from the American attorney general, Jeff Sessions, defending the separation of parents and their children coming to the United States, and citing a Bible verse—

RW: What was the verse?

GG: From Romans. [Romans 13:1] "Subject yourself . . ."

RW: Oh, to the authorities.

GG: To the authorities. We would make this caution in any case, that no one verse can stand for the whole Bible any more than one line can stand for a book, a novel, a poem even.

RW: Indeed.

GG: One of the things that was very heartening for me about the response to that statement was first that people talked about how scripture has to be read in its context, including its original context. You know, why does Paul say this? Well, why does Paul say anything? Because he is trying to speak to a circumstance, and it may not be every circumstance. He's speaking in a particular power structure and trying to situate Christianity within a particular power structure. What was heartening to me was how many Christian groups (including evangelical Christians, who have been allies to this administration, largely) simply said that that's not the message the Bible has for us. It's not this one thing you can use to justify anything the government does. It has been used in previous governments to do so. What about those thousands of verses about what Jesus called "the least of these"? What are we supposed to do with those people out of power, who God seems to look on most favorably because they are the people who most need our care?

RW: Yes. Yes, the people whose voices are being silenced. It's back to this question of what is the human dignity that scripture lays out, as God's fundamental will and purpose for us? All of that rests on the assumption that the human is what God loves passionately. The human is what God looks on with delight, as God looks with delight on the whole of creation of course, but very specifically that image of God's being which humanity is. You therefore have to ask, is this or that behavior, this or that policy, making it harder or easier for us to imagine the human as the object of God's passion and delight? And I think where you have children in cages, the answer is actually a no-brainer. Or indeed where you have, as in both our countries unfortunately, penal policies which are systematically unjust, degrading. Unjust in terms of class and race. Degrading in terms of conditions and attitudes around them, and degrading to our politics overall because the issue is repeatedly ignored and swept under the carpet.

GG: Yes. One thing, and it's not a justification certainly but an explanation for it, is that we often make our moral and ethical decisions, even when we're people of faith, less out of our faith traditions than we do out of our partisan politics and our identities in those.

RW: And our economic position.

GG: And our economic position. I did an experiment for *Patheos* [patheos.com] back from 2010–2012, where for two years I did this very strange and disorienting thing. In writing about current events and the politics of the day, I tried to set aside my beliefs as a card-carrying Democrat and, as unencumbered as I could by the set of filters that all of us are encumbered by, to come back to the issue, and to look at the tradition, to look at the Fathers, to look at the teaching of the Episcopal Church, and to ask myself, does this in any way change the way that I think about this issue? And in some occasions it did. [The result was a book, *Faithful Citizenship*, 2012.] And I found that, just to give the easiest and most controversial example: as a Democrat, I had always believed in abortion as a sort of fundamental right, and I found my continuing belief that abortion is sometimes necessary to be very much complicated by the ethic of life that Christianity calls for. I had never stopped to consider that because in the Democratic party right now, to suggest that abortion be limited even, in any way, is—

RW: A sin against the Holy Ghost.

GG: Yes, it's a sin against the Holy Ghost. And there are comparable offences on the right.

RW: Yes. Yes, and that's a real eye-opener about the tribalism of our politics, and the way in which we approach our politics with package deals. If you are, in American terms, in favor of gun control, you are obviously in favor of universally available abortion, and vice versa, you'd think. What's the slogan I've occasionally seen in the States? *Pro Life, Pro Guns, Pro God*. And I think, pardon?

GG: Yes.

RW: Maybe only two of those.

GG: Yes, I see the possible dilemma there.

RW: Yes. It must have been about twenty years ago, the late Cardinal [Joseph] Bernardin of Chicago [archbishop of Chicago from 1982–1996] was among those who launched what was meant to be a sort of comprehensive, joined-up approach to pro-life issues, which brought in questions about the death penalty, about the management of arms, and so forth, along with the traditional questions about abortion or about euthanasia. It seems to me that unless you make those joining-up of things not as a package deal, not as a set of tribal attitudes that are prescribed but as things that are genuinely linked together, really the moral discourse withers away. And the abortion question is certainly one of those where I'd say that we have demonstrated our great reluctance or inability to live with an imperfect moral vision. We haven't been able to sustain the idea that abortion is genuinely the taking of a human life, therefore genuinely a tragic event of loss generally speaking, and that there are conditions where perhaps the only thing that sustains the human dignity of a woman in those situations is the possibility of a termination, which is a very uncomfortable place to be when you've got absolutists bellowing in each ear.

GG: Right, right.

RW: Yet it seems to me that that's a recognition of the fact that we are not saved just by keeping rules, whether liberal or conservative.

GG: I wonder if this feels true for you here in England, but I think another of the problems that we have in this discourse about public life is that in America we often tend to think of it in terms of rights—

RW: Ah, yes.

GG: —as opposed to what I think in Christian terms we might think about as responsibilities. Because America has these rights that are enshrined in our foundational documents and that are assumed to sort of flow out—

RW: Yes.

GG: —into other places in the culture, where basically you are encouraged to make the most room for yourself, with the expectation that your rights are not going to be impinged on. That's a large part of our mythology. It's the open skies, it's the American West, it's the frontier do-as-you-please.

RW: Yes. But it's also something that affects the entire North Atlantic cultural world. Even in terms of the primary school which says to the child, "You can be anything you want to be." My heart goes out there because I fully understand that you might want to say to a child in a primary, sorry, elementary school, "Nothing is impossible for you." Because they don't understand their own potential, their own dignity, their own richness. And yet, a responsible education does also say to people, "You can't be anything you want." There are things like *you*, the person you (and any person) are, with the limits, the weaknesses, that just go with being a person. If you go through life imagining that what is owed to you is infinite possibility, you are heading for disaster, the wreckage of yourself and everybody around you. So how an educationist walks that line is a real challenge. To allow people to fail, which increasingly we're not very good at in our educational systems (as well as in otherwise)—

GG: No.

RW: To allow people to fail is the most humane thing we can do sometimes. To say, yes, this is wrong, or this is inadequate, this is a failure, and that's not the end of your world or mine.

GG: Right. One of the places where I find that that language is really important for us in the States is in the gun-control argument. It does sort of seem to be binary; it's all of it or none of it. I come from a family that has guns, that shoots, that hunts. I don't have a gun, right now, because I'm also embracing that Christian pacifism.

RW: I'm pleased to note, as we speak.

GG: But many people that I love do have guns, and it does not make them bad people. There's first this assumption across that binary divide that the person with whom we disagree is fundamentally different from us, bad in some way. But I think there is that possibility, if we move back from the rights discourse to the responsibility discourse that's embedded in our tradition, that we can say, even if your right to have a gun is enshrined in our Constitution, is it possible that there is some point where you should embrace the responsibility of saying, "Is it a good thing for everyone to have a gun? Is it a good thing for everyone to have lots of guns? Is it a good thing for everyone to have lots of guns and as many bullets as they can fire out of a large magazine?" And the sort of conclusion that I came to in that experiment was that even though I personally support people having guns in a responsible way, as a Christian I also see the need to limit my freedom because it causes harm to my brother and sister.

RW: Which is simply a paraphrase of what St. Paul says in Romans, isn't it [Romans 14]? We just don't read that intelligently very often. Paul says, "Of course the food laws are irrelevant to your reconciliation with God. But the food laws may not be irrelevant to the message you are giving out to your fellow Christian." And if you go around saying, "Keeping the food laws is just a sign of how spiritually immature you are," then you know, time to go back to keeping kosher because you are just treading on the other person who is the object of God's passion and delight.

And the gun question, I suppose for us over in the UK, is one of the most deeply baffling cultural elements of the United States. Like most of us, I have to be honest that I cannot see the logic of widespread gun possession. Absolutely cannot see it. I can understand it historically, in terms of a militia-oriented society, but is that the truth today? And it's perfectly true, of course, as some people say, that stricter gun controls don't prevent violence and murder. It's perfectly true that people kill people, guns don't. But the blindingly obvious question to me is, "So what are the conditions which make gun ownership a major threat to society, a major destabilizing element?" Of course, again, as we've been reminded, knives kill as well as guns do. But the question is, "What makes that possible? What makes that a way of life that people sign up for, what makes that a strategy people resort to?"

GG: Right.

RW: So it's important, I think, to put all of these questions, whether it's gun control, or abortion, whatever, into a social context. You have a social context where gun ownership is a really, or potentially, deeply destabilizing thing. Well, what's the issue should be obvious. If you put abortion into a context where terminations are disproportionately a matter for disadvantaged, disempowered women in impoverished social backgrounds, might you not think about what would make that a less attractive option for someone?

GG: We were talking, I think the other day, about how neither of our governments at this time seems capable of governing.

RW: Absolutely.

GG: And we have these huge issues separating us. And they're not all the same issues, but there's very much the sense that our leaders and our legislatures don't seem to be able to tackle these problems in any sort of way. In the States, we see that as largely a function of what it takes you to get elected, and the primary system which polarizes so dramatically and makes it impossible to govern with any sort of consensus because you have your constituents back home who have sent you to Washington or wherever, and they will not stand for compromise. And yet, what we often hear is that governance is the art of the imperfect.

RW: Yes. That's why I think the solution to our real crisis of democracy at the moment is probably encouraging people to get more experience in hands-on democracy. What does it actually take to run a town, or a district? If people are elected to office in a district of the city or something like that, what makes that work? You have to do deals with the other people who will not go away. You have to consider what's achievable. You have to consider whether you will sacrifice the achievable for the perfect and therefore leave everybody pretty much where they were to start with. And that's the routine business of the local government, or even, for that matter, the government of a school, a golf club.

GG: Yes, any sort of governance.

RW: We all know that, yet mysteriously when it's elevated another layer up, we forget that, and we behave as if it were a zero-sum game. Now, drawing out on the actual experiences of people, making things work, is, I think, a much better strategy than just trading slogans. Getting more people to talk about their experience of having to govern, to run things, which so many people do have, and the point at which they will say, "This is what I have to do in order to make things work." The bizarre thing is, you have a president who talks about his skills as a deal-maker.

GG: A negotiator, yes.

RW: I don't see that in spades, I have to say. I think what he means is that he is somebody with some experience of getting results in the business world. But that's not actually governing, because you don't simply have to craft a deal, you have to make a program that people can cooperate with, sign up to, move forward with. And that's what we all seem to be afraid of, and in this country too, where the polarization of political discourse has just reached a very grim point. I'm not one of those who thinks that it's worse than ever. I was reviewing a book recently about the struggles around Catholic emancipation in the UK in the early nineteenth century [Antonia Fraser, *The King and the Catholics: The Fight for Rights, 1829*, 2018], and there were points where I looked up from the book and said, "Goodness, we think *we've* got problems." But what is illuminating is that you look at these historical mirrors and you see some of the same pathologies coming through: the demonization of others, the refusal for a long time to imagine there could be another way of doing things. And then the drip, drip, drip, gradual recognition, *this has got to work*. This has got to be operative in such a way that it doesn't stop the trains running on time. This has got to work in such a way that children grow up safely. And slowly, people come around to saying, "Yes, we will have to find something we can all put our names to." That's one of the dangers, isn't it, of the campaign-style rhetoric that we take for granted now? I remember thinking during—well, during both elections, yours and ours recently—given the high temperature of the controversy during the campaign, whoever gets elected will have got elected on the back of so delegitimizing the other side that it would make no sense to collaborate with them. If these people are the demons—

GG: Right.

RW: —vile, evil, antipatriotic, all the passion and commitment that we've been saying they are for the last six months, why on earth should I offer to do a deal with them? Which is why I respect those, again, in your system and ours, who are prepared to say, "Yes, I disagree fundamentally with so-and-so, but I can respect where they're coming from, and I have a sense of how I might be able to find common ground." And in all the great moments, and there haven't been that many, sadly, in the last fifty years or so, where a little bit of light has appeared after decades of conflict—Northern Ireland, South Africa—it's been those moments where people have somehow found the capacity to look at one another and say, "You are still a stranger, you are still in some ways an enemy, but I know that together we have got to make this work for everybody else, because we are not important enough to dictate everybody else's fate, we have to make this a society that is livable here."

GG: It reminds me, you talked about the sort of bright spots, of which there have been so few of late. I was thinking about the convention rallies of the last election cycle [2016] in America, and often, as you said, how hateful, how charged the rhetoric was. And I was thinking of a general election a ways back, where our Senator McCain, John McCain, was a presidential candidate, and one of the delegitimizing pieces of rhetoric about Barack Obama was that he was from another country, he was a secret Muslim, he was all of these things. We have had more recent candidates who not only would have encouraged people to speculate on that, but would have started those controversies.

RW: Naming no names.

GG. Naming none. But I remember a rally at which this woman got up and asked McCain a question and started saying terrible things about Barack Obama, about how he wasn't fit to govern America, he wasn't American, any of those things. And McCain stopped her. A lot of our readers will remember this, because it stands out for many of us. He said, "You know, I disagree with him fundamentally about how our country should be run. But I believe he is a good human being, a decent human being. I don't want to listen to this defamation of his character."

RW: I remember that moment, and I wish that could be run on continuous loop, really.

GG: That seems to be one of the things that we're called to, those of us who are in power, those of us who want to speak back to power, that reminder that, as you were saying, we are all in this together, we are all a part of this human experiment. We are all children of God, and God loves you just as much as He does me, even though we have these fundamental disagreements.

RW: That's right. The sense that there is genuinely a common human project means that I cannot, finally, isolate my good or my hope from yours. They've got to be convergent somewhere along the line.

GG: Yes.

RW: And that can be a very long way along the line, but that's our faith, and that surely is what, again, what the New Testament lunges us toward, in saying that the optimal human community, the body of Christ, is one where it is absolutely basic that everyone's destiny is tied up with everybody else's.

But I think also this brings us back to some of our earlier conversations about language, and we talked about responsibility, which belongs to those of us who have faith in this setting, but also the responsibility that rests on those of us who use language, imaginatively or creatively. And I think it's an important part of seeing this as a genuine vocation, that we are called on somehow to do things with language that are not weaponized. To use language in a way that looks for recognition, that opens rather than closes doors. And that's not, again, to back away from conflict in all circumstances, or to say, "Well, if everybody just talked to each other the world would be nicer." It is to say we have a task to work at language to show its complexity, to show its diverse, rich relationship to the reality of our relations, rather than just treating it as yet another means of diminishing or disempowering others. There's a real morality about writing, I think.

GG: And that counts for any of the kinds of writing that we do as people of faith. I have, as you do, various ways that I push writing out into the world. We talked about the pulpit earlier, we both write essays and articles and op-ed pieces, and I think you're absolutely right that we have this responsibility to convey that whatever our disagreements, we have this powerful sense that there are still more ways that we are alike than unalike. And that we seek these goods that Bonhoeffer would have told us are the things around which we can somehow find agreement. Where that happened in the States, the week before this conversation, was in the immigration policy separating children from their parents at the border. People who had been on all sides of the issue on immigration said that this is absolutely wrong. Whatever we feel about people coming to this country, or the conditions under which they come, this is an absolute violation of their humanity. And we can agree on this even though we may not agree about everything around this issue.

RW: Yes. A crucially important moment, I think. Because again it comes back to what sort of humanity are you seeing and serving here, and what kind of model of humanity is served by tearing a child away from its parents. No good saying, "Well, that's what the law says," because in that case, clearly there's something wrong with the law. Certainly with the way you're administrating it.

GG: I've been thinking about [Henry David] Thoreau a lot the last few weeks. I often teach *Civil Disobedience* [1849], and there are all these wonderful pieces connected there: there's [Thomas] Aquinas talking about unjust laws, and you move forward from Thoreau to [Mahatma] Gandhi, and then you've got [Martin Luther] King in this line of people reflecting on the law, and what makes a law a law worth following. I'm thinking right now about what it is that people of faith can do when they see a law that is manifestly un-Christian. Both here and in the States, I know there have been lots of demonstrations. I expect when our president shows up [in the UK] next week, if he shows his face in public, there will be a number of people reflecting—

RW: I shouldn't be surprised.

GG: —some animosity back toward him. But I wonder, what can people of faith do, particularly at a time when they don't feel like their political systems answer to them?

RW: Indeed. And also at a time when they feel their own moral credibility has been undermined, in some ways, by failure and misconduct. I think in this country, and Ireland, and to some extent in the States and Australia, the whole miserable history of collusion in sexual abuse has undermined the church's moral credibility in a range of areas.

GG: Right.

RW: Although we hope and pray the worst practice is a thing of the past, the shadow is a long one. So yes, it won't do just to say, "We *are* the moral compass," because people will say, "Really?" and point to the record.

GG: What about this, and this.

RW: But I think what we can say sometimes is—to go back to the way I put it just now—what we can say is to pose the question, "What kind of humanity does this serve? If you do this, what does that show about your attitude to the human?" And I think it's perfectly right that Christians in so many denominations can say, if we have colluded with or not taken seriously enough the reality of sexual abuse of children or vulnerable people, then clearly the message we have given out is that their humanity is of no interest to us. And that's the message that people have received and, quite rightly, turned against. So, if we are honest about our repentance here, maybe we can be heard a bit more clearly. Again, that's something I keep coming back to. Repentance as something other than the mark of failure. Repentance is something which is helpful. It's the ability to say, I did this, I failed in this way, and I know that that did not kill me, because I know I have a Redeemer. I have a Divine Lover that does not let me off, or blot out what I've done, but says, "Now let's work through these consequences for your life rather than for your death, shall we?"

GG: The great model for us in the States, of course, is the nonviolent civil rights movement.

RW: Of course.

GG: And Dr. King was the most visible figure in a nation-wide movement. This is the fiftieth anniversary, as we're talking here in 2018, of Dr. King's death. He is remembered now for the successes, most of them taking place in the American South, in a cultural setting where he was able to operate in a different way than in the Northern cities. We also forget that when he started taking on other issues—when he took on economics, poverty, the Vietnam War—that it was harder to gather a coalition around those things, even though he saw—

RW: He saw a connection.

GG: He saw a connection between all of them. And the thing that I think about now, as we reflect on the fiftieth anniversary of what we think of as the great success of a Christian movement in politics, is that when King died, he really thought of himself as a failure.

RW: As a failure.

GG: That had he lived longer, we might think of him differently than we do. Yet it feels to me that the lesson he gave, that nonviolent mobilization of, of failure, as you put it, he gave as the Christian model.

RW: Yes.

GG: As unsexy as it is, as unwinning as it is in this zero-sum game that politics has become, for me that's still the compelling model for what we're called to do.

RW: Yes. Yes. It's to do with witness, which as I grow older I come to see as a more and more fundamental category. Bearing witness. It is possible to live like this, indeed die like this. It's possible. And just to do it, never mind the impact, never mind the output. Just to do it, says, "This is real." And again, that connects back with some of what we were saying about Shakespeare, doesn't it? The tragic. It's not that you're looking for a happy ending, but you're looking for some contact with what is essential, what is real. Certainly one of the things that moves me most about Martin Luther King's legacy, as he described it, is—well what comes to mind is Paul's words: "I was not disobedient in the heavenly calling" [Acts 26:19]. As if throughout his life, he was aware of a calling to witness, and he never said no. He was a flawed man. He was not always a wise man. But he was a faithful man, in that respect.

GG: Yes, and we talk about *faithful to the end*.

RW: We do.

GG: That last speech of Dr. King's in Memphis, which is, to my mind, maybe the most powerful, because he is thinking very much about his death ["I've Been to the Mountaintop," April 3, 1968]. That speech begins with his—it was a fairly routine sort of thing, because there had been a bomb threat, and so they had searched the plane, and the baggage, and the plane was delayed because of that. I think that we forget that for most of the years of his adult life, King lived with that level of threat. And in fact, his house was bombed. There was this potential for violence, and for his witness to end, as it ultimately did, and yet he showed up every single day, imperfect as he was in some other ways. To live as faithful a life as that is an incredible witness.

RW: Yes. That's the gift to the life of the body that he has made and still makes. And I think too—well, I have both their pictures up there—King and Oscar Romero. Romero is being canonized this fall.

GG: Yes.

RW: Thank the Lord.

GG: You know, King makes me think of the other sort of response that the church can make at a time when there is this discord in the body politic. It is our responsibility to confront, to confront the unjust laws and to call us to better behaviors, drawn out of our understanding through the tradition. But it's also comfort. It's not just a temporal comfort, although I take comfort in the solidarity that exists among my faith community, there are these things that we agree are not acceptable and we can work together toward them. But it also goes back to the larger redemptive question that you brought up, which is, whatever is happening in this present moment, however sin and death are manifesting themselves in the world at this moment, that battle is won.

RW: Yes. Yes.

GG: If we can just remember that. That is the heart of what we understand. And as King said in that final speech, I may not see it, which is the tragic irony of his delivering that speech the night before he died, but it's also the reality. Because none of us ever really sees it. We see movement. A movement here, a movement there. I think of Archbishop [Desmond] Tutu, who is one of the great figures of the past hundred years in reconciliation, and the places where movement still needs to happen in his country and around the world. But there is an incredible comfort to know that in the cosmic sense, we are loved and valued and redeemed, regardless of what is on the front page of the *New York Times* today.

RW: Yes, indeed. *The fight is o'er, the battle done, now is the victor's triumph won* ["The Strife is O'er, the Battle Done," translated by Francis Pott]. That's the Easter proclamation, and far from its being a statement that everything is all right *really*, it says, everything is not all right, but is beneath the hands of God, specifically the wounded hands of Christ, and there is nothing that can extinguish that divine fidelity to us. When we're thinking about the comfort the church gives, I think the most important thing, very often, we can give, is that embodied assurance that people are not alone, they're not abandoned.

GG: Right.

RW: That's another form of just turning up, you and I know, that often pastorally the only thing we can do is to be there for someone, without words. When the church is present in a community of deprivation and struggle and suffering, in our countries, or South Sudan, or the Solomon Islands, or Brazil, or wherever, what it's saying is, "You, this community, you are worth spending time with. God spends God's time with you. And the church spends God's time with you, and in you, and among you." And there's the hope, that what we are connected to in that moment is something whose potential and possibility can never be extinguished. And what do we say but "Hallelujah."

Conversation Seven

In Which Rowan and Greg Discuss: The Church at This Time / Institutionality and Relationality in the Church / Church as Every Day / Welsh Community / Hope for the Church / The Shifting Manifestation of the Church / Sacraments / What Is Saving Your Life Now?

RW: So our question was about where we see ourselves in the church at the moment.

GG: Yes. What is giving you hope? What would you like to see? Naturally, people are interested. After ten years of wrangling cats, you've had plenty of time to think.

RW: That's right. In the ten years of being archbishop, I suppose I was conscious of the fact that my job, or part of my job, was inescapably institutional. I had to try and make the structures work. By the end of my time, I think I was fairly convinced that a lot of the structures were not going to work in the way that they had, if they ever had. What was emerging was a much more lateral and relational pattern of connection within the Anglican family, and that maybe it would not be the end of the world if some of the complex administrative structures we had buckled under the strain of conflict. I'm not saying it's a good thing for that to happen, but not, perhaps, lethal.

One reason, I guess, I resisted simply letting the Communion dissolve was simply that I know from history that churches fracture more quickly than they heal, and I didn't think this is a time when we could afford to let much visible fracture happen. Not for institutional reasons but just because in this polarized, feverish environment we live in at the moment, it's probably a recipe for just deepening conflicts and running further and further towards the corner of the room. So, I don't think it was a complete waste of time trying to make those structures work, but I am aware that the life is coming in other ways.

I think the thing I look back on, in my time as archbishop, with most satisfaction, if you're allowed to say that, is putting together the Anglican Alliance [Anglican aid and partnership network, founded in 2010] in the last year or two. That's to say, the network of relief and development agencies across the Communion which is still going, and still going quite strong. Because that was one of several new kinds of alignment and connection which suggested how we might go on talking with each other and working with each other, even when, you know, the great beasts of the jungle were bellowing their way through the thickets and trampling all before them.

Meanwhile, things go on. I could mention various kinds of theological networks in the Communion—the sheer fact of diocese to diocese, parish to parish, relationship across the Communion—and think, that's where the actual flow of blood is, and it doesn't just depend on getting the structures right. So that gives me hope. But what also gives me hope is simply being here in this environment, in a university where there is a surprising amount of sympathy and curiosity about the Christian faith, in a college where, thanks to brilliant pastoral work by some of my colleagues, the vitality of the Christian community is very, very visible. Little churches around here in the city and in the countryside, I visit and think, people have a real appetite to grow as believers. It's that appetite to grow that I sense in so many areas. You'll know something of what I mean: you came into a congregation, as I understand, which had that appetite, and you were able both to be fed and to feed. I think that's still a part of the way you see yourself, is it not?

GG: Absolutely. What gives me hope, surprisingly, is I think also in that lateral and relational concept that you talked about. It's not that there are not a number of wonderful gifts that our tradition has, because, obviously, we find that a lot of younger Christians are drawn to the liturgy. Back in the States, my friend Rachel Held Evans, who had been one of the best-known evangelical figures in the States, made that sort of journey to the Episcopal tradition to where she felt philosophically she was more closely paired, but also it was a liturgical decision. This was a way that she felt God speaking to her. I feel that those are some of our resources: the beauty of our worship, the beauty of the language (we've talked about language a lot). But in the book that I did about the Episcopal Church and the Anglican tradition and where it's going [*My Church Is Not Dying: Episcopalians in the 21st Century*, Morehouse, 2015], I noticed that the last couple of chapters were a lot about new ways of being relational—

RW: Yes. Yes.

GG: —about reaching outside the walls of the church and finding appropriate partners in the communities and in people who may never set foot in our churches, which is totally against the model that we have where we measure how many people are in a pew on Sunday morning. I feel lucky that two of the bishops I know well, my own bishop from Texas, Andy Doyle, and Greg Rickel have sort of set up this model about *church is every day*. It's about reaching out to people around the clock, finding ways of doing the work of peace and justice and reconciliation, as well as the beautiful worship we do. That brings me a lot of hope, because there are a lot of success stories in the church here and in the American church, where those kinds of relationships are advancing the causes that we care so much about.

RW: Yes. Looking back to my time when I was working in Wales, one of the great beacons of light there was the community of Penrhys in the Rhondda Valley. Penrhys is a village on a hillside overlooking the Rhondda Valley. It was the place where all the problem families and the criminal groups from Cardiff were deported, as it were—

GG: So, Australia.

RW: —to live in this wretched council estate, public housing estate, as you'd say. Well, it was a chaotic community, deprived in every possible way. And a minister from the United Reformed Church

[Reverend Dr. John Morgan] decided that he and his wife would go to live on the estate, and just see what could be done to create a church. So they bought up two battered little properties, and lived in half of that as a house, and cleared the space for a worship center, a secondhand clothes shop, and a café drop-in center. They ministered there for seventeen years, I think.

GG: Wow.

RW: The building of community was fragile, and often interrupted. People came and went, the tides rose and fell, but the networks developed all the time. So, for example, relations were built with churches in Eastern Europe. Also, relations were built with the Roman Catholic Trappist community on Caldey Island [Caldey Abbey], who sent a bell for the church center. And they just carried on witnessing through all that. John Morgan is the minister who organized it, a very great man indeed. John had a vision of the church catholic, as you might say, which seemed to me an absolutely classical, mainstream Christian vision. This was a sacramental worshiping community, set down in the midst of the human world, whose task was to absolve, enrich, enhance, reconcile, where it was. And for all those years, until the majority of the houses were at last demolished, that's how that little center worked.

GG: Wow.

RW: I used to say of that what whoever it was [New York reporter Lincoln Joseph Steffens] said about the Soviet Union, in the twenties, so stupidly: "I have seen the future and it works." I have seen the church, and it works. It's that kind of thing that makes me think, God continues to call and sustain the church catholic, and that when we're promised that the gates of hell will not prevail, it's not that God has promised Christ and the great sort-of juggernaut of the Church will finally squash all opposition and reign supreme. It's that there's finally no human situation that could hold out against the gospel. The gates of hell shall not prevail. That is, the gates, the defenses, of darkness, destruction, loss, cannot finally resist, so there's nowhere the body can't be.

GG: You'll remember that the title of that book that I wrote about our tradition was *My Church Is Not Dying*, which the publisher thought was a really lovely and sort of catchy title. I was properly brought to task by one of the folks that I interviewed for the book, which is full of stories about where people are finding life in the Episcopal and Anglican traditions. First, he sort of gently took me to task by saying, "It's not your church, Greg. It's Jesus's church."

RW: Yes, okay. Hands up!

GG: And I was like, "Yes, I do remember that." And he said, "And of course it's not dying." His point exactly was that it cannot. You know, our particular manifestations, the human institutions, they're our interfacing with Jesus, who has established something which is much bigger than any of us, and which goes on in some form or other, and which changes as we look back through history.

RW: Of course.

GG: Whatever it's going to be one hundred years from now may not look much like what we see now, but there's that movement.

RW: And what's interesting in the history, of course, is (as before I spoke about tides rising and falling), some things prove themselves by their durability, by their coming back. So I would say that two hundred years ago, the Anglican world, and most of the Protestant world, would have been sacramentally minimal. We wouldn't go to Holy Communion very often, it wouldn't be celebrated very often. But gradually, the sense of the absolutely focal character of the sacrament of the Lord's Supper has crept back in all these places. Gradually people have rediscovered why it might have mattered to be there, in the body, worshiping at that particular level, in that particular way. Traditions of prayer which had slipped away have slipped back. Some things which once would have been absolutely obvious have slipped away. But some things just seem to reaffirm themselves, age after age.

And that gives me hope, certainly, that there is an energy, a— what's the word—a drive, say, in the church, which takes us back to that fundamental mystery, baptism and Eucharist, and the Paschal event, and the rest of it. Even in our own lifetime, certainly in my lifetime a bit more than yours, I look back on how we celebrated Holy Week and Easter when I was a boy, and how much richer that celebration now is, as if we've recovered something that we'd lost sight of, and realized, we have to make the most of this.

GG: That's lovely. I know Episcopalians in whose living memory that sacramental tradition has changed. They talk about how they did Morning Prayer every Sunday. Of course, as someone who came into the church, at least in large part, because of that sacramental moment and because of the encounter with Jesus that I felt in every communion, it's hard to even fathom. As much as I like Morning Prayer, that would not have been a compelling reason for me to become Episcopalian, or maybe even Christian. But encountering Jesus every week at the altar most definitely was. That's a wonderful example of strong and positive change.

RW: Which I think means that if we see the church changing in front of us (and sometimes we see the church changing in ways we don't very much like), the message is, don't panic. He's not going anywhere.

GG: It also puts me in mind of the sermon that Bono gave at the American National Prayer Breakfast a few years ago. He talked about a wise man who told him, "Bono, I've noticed that you're always praying to God. And you're always praying that God will get on board with what you're doing. Why don't you ask God what God wants to do, and get on board with that?" And that struck me as pretty good advice.

RW: That's very good advice, very good advice. The definition of mission, which I've so often heard, and so often repeated is: finding out what God is doing, and joining in.

GG: Yes. So I think the last thing that I'd like to explore with you as we finish up this conversation comes from my friend Barbara Brown Taylor's sort of constant question to find out where God is moving in our lives. She likes to ask, "What is saving your life now?" I wonder if there is a thing, or two, or three, that you could isolate at this moment, in 2018, in which something, someone, God, is saving your life right now?

RW: I'd say the experience of being in this particular college community for the last few years has been a lifesaver. I realized in the first six months or so of doing this job just how much baggage of tiredness, pain, reproach, sense of failure, frustration I was carrying from the years of being archbishop. To be simply a member of a community like this—okay, with a responsibility, but a member of a community where conversations are possible. That's been a lifesaver, and continues to be. And I hope that whatever lies ahead beyond this particular situation, that will still be true. So that's certainly one thing. And connected with that I guess is the experience of ministering regularly in a couple of small churches, not for big events or special events, but discovering again what it is to preach to the same community over a period of time, not just doing a kind of hit-and-run exercise as a visiting celebrity or something.

GG: Right. Visiting and vaulting out.

RW: Those two things, I suppose, those are really springs of life. And you?

GG: This will not surprise you, but one of the things that is saving my life now is my family and my marriage. You have known me before and after. I was unhappily married, and each marriage ended more unhappily than the one before it. I was single for many, many years, and I thought that I would never love again, and never know love again. You wrote so beautifully in "The Body's Grace" [lecture given in 1989, now collected in *Theology and Sexuality: Classic and Contemporary Readings*, Blackwell, 2002] about how we understand and apprehend God's love through the love of another human being, whose touch we experience. And you will remember actually praying alongside me about what to do, as I fell in love with a dear friend, who is now my wife, Jeanie.

There were moments where it felt like I was in a situation comedy, or a romantic comedy. It's like, *I'm in love with my friend, should*

I tell her? Should I not tell her? How should I tell her? Should I write her a note? And as overwrought as the situation seems in my memory, it was the absolute thing that had to happen. It happened at the precise time that it was supposed to happen. And all of that unhappiness, and the grief of relationships past, where I was so sick, and so unavailable, has been transformed by the love that I have found, and the love that I have for Jeanie and for our girls. It is a daily remembrance and thankfulness.

RW: It's wonderful to see. And to see how, again, you have been fed and are feeding, in that setting.

GG: And then, I think maybe the other thing that is feeding me is we've talked a lot about writing. I am just finishing a novel, and it's a very good novel. And as much as I like the work that I do for the church, and the theological interpretation that I do, there is this very powerful sense that even though I may have carved a niche for myself as someone talking about religion and culture, as with you, as a poet and playwright, there are some things that only I can do.

RW: Yes.

GG: And God has given me, if you will, this particular charge to tell these particular stories, and whatever audience out there that might need them will find them. So particularly at this moment, I am giving thanks for the opportunity to be an artist, to create, for the gift of whatever talent I possess, and the prayer for faithfulness, that I will honor that gift. But those two things are very central for me. The ongoing thing (and we almost do not need to talk about the Church, and the faithful relationship to it) is that I do continue to give thanks for the Episcopal Church. Flawed as it is, as every human institution is, the love and acceptance that I've experienced there I know is echoed by many people who have come into the Episcopal Church in recent years. So I would say the Episcopal Church is also saving my life, every day.

RW: Praise be.

Afterword

WHAT'S FASCINATING—even moving—about reading the finished text of this book is to watch new thoughts emerging in the process of speaking and listening. I think that both Greg and I would recognize that rather strange feeling of "I didn't know I knew that" which comes with really good conversation. And of course without the conversation, I *wouldn't* have known that. There's actually very little that we discover as human beings on our own—certainly very little indeed that's of serious human significance.

As it happens, I'm writing this on the day after taking part in an event organized by the "Inspire Dialogue" Foundation, which is dedicated to promoting discussion of public ethics and spiritual resources. Our title was "Difficult Conversations"; the centerpiece of it was a conversation between two people from different ethnic backgrounds in Rwanda, one of them a survivor of the 1990s genocide, the other the daughter of a leading figure in the government at the time of the genocide. It was a very intense encounter, sometimes demanding or even painful for the hearers as well as the participants. But what the two very courageous and honest Rwandans said was that they felt able to probe one another and challenge one another because they were confident that the group as a whole was guaranteeing their safety; they conversed like this because they trusted not only one another but the "shared world" of the group, or the shared *culture* of the group. They recognized that the habits and protocols and existing relationships within the group would not tolerate threats, evasions, or manipulation. The outcome was both a deeply moving and significant conversation, and a set of proposals for next steps in relationship-building, individual and collective, involving some of the wider community who had witnessed this meeting of hearts.

There would be lots of similar stories from diverse contexts that would parallel this. It seems that discovery and change happen when we feel secure enough, not only with each other, but with a wider world that we have come to inhabit, a "culture" in which there is an expectation of being gifted by the process, being stretched but also enriched, because both speakers know that they are in a place where something more is at work, something more is being acknowledged than just the history and experience of two individuals. It's as if—if we want to be in touch with the deepest places in ourselves—we need not just another person to reflect back to us or argue with us, but a broader landscape which neither of us *owns* but which both of us find habitable. That wider landscape invites, prompts, and nourishes in all sorts of ways, so that the cues and hints we let fall for each other in talking can be enlarged beyond what we thought was possible. And if all goes well and blessedly, we end up touching something very basic in each other; as someone put it, you make contact with each other's deepest *wants*: you bring to light what each other is longing for, beyond any ideas of winning an argument or even finding a common agenda of interests.

This is a fair way from a conversation between two writers with academic interests and Christian commitments, however lively and generative of new ideas. But I think that understanding of what real conversation involves in this very fraught and weighted context may help us see that this activity, conversation, which seems so routine and ordinary, becomes transformative because of all sorts of things that are larger than two people alone. Greg and I have found over the years that our shared enthusiasms for both writing and theology have mapped out a landscape where we can probe and explore, share and confess (in every sense of that resourceful word!) what makes sense to us, and *of* us; and in that process, we find that the shared world of imagination and spirit which we have identified as a world that both of us love and trust is increasingly letting each of us see more of ourselves as well as of the other.

So this book is in a way a celebration of that common world—not a world of universally identical taste or judgement or belief, but a world where difference in these things can be seen as a gift, a new kind of serious and joyful apprehension of where and who we are, a way of being and seeing that unfolds a new perspective on the familiar. I began with the still very raw memory of a "difficult" conversation. The times Greg and I shared in speaking together were never difficult like that; but what perhaps makes the exchanges of our friendship and our delight in each other worth setting down is the simple fact that they illustrate one way in which conversation can be *discovery*. And if we know that this is possible, we know that the last word does not belong to the merchants of zero-sum games, to those who talk for victory and for the humiliation and silencing of the other. When that happens, as it does so much in our increasingly insane political world, fueled by the infantilism that flourishes in corners of the online "community," we can be sure that people have turned their backs on any hope of a shared world. And this in turn means that they have turned their backs on the idea that there is a truth and a hope more solid than anything an individual ego can sustain: the world shrinks to the scale of my own experience and conviction and drive for power. We desperately need cultures and institutions of shared meaning that allow space for patient talking and listening because they let us see something of a horizon that is not just "yours" or "mine." For us as Christians, it is quite simply the space into which the mystery of God invites us—that sacred space that isn't anyone's property, but is somewhere where unlikely people can find a home together. The Reign of God, which Jesus promises and embodies is surely just that space, where transformation happens because we have moved away, even if only just a little bit, from the terrible standoff of rival egos, and have started to sense what it might be to gaze together into the mystery of God and God's world, turning to one another gladly from time to time to say, "Look at that!"

Rowan Williams
September 2018